Transforming Traumatic Grief

Six Steps to Move from Grief to Peace
After the Sudden or Violent Death of a Loved One

Courtney Armstrong
M. Ed., LPC

Published by Artemecia Press

ISBN: 0983499918
ISBN-13: 9780983499916
LCCN: 2011905776

Authors Note

Cases described in this book are composites of typical client stories. Some stories have been combined and names or other identifying details have been changed to protect the privacy of the individuals and families.

Although this book offers tools to help you through the grief process, it is not a substitute for professional help. Please contact a mental health professional if you need additional support.

Contents

Dedications

Joel, thank you for your infinite love, patience and support. Tu auras toujours mon coeur.

Jon Connelly, your brilliant work has pulled so many of us out of darkness, and you are a light to the world.

Tara, my dearest friend and the most resilient woman I know. May you and David continue following your bliss.

Margie, you amaze me with your courage, perseverance, and sense of humor. May you receive as many blessings as you've given to others.

Acknowledgments

My enduring gratitude also goes out to the following people who helped bring this book to life:

My editor, Cindy Barrilleaux, who believed in this project and helped me find my voice. Bill O'Hanlon for spurring me on, teaching me the value of persistence, and sharing my passion for positive psychology approaches. Melinda Lucanese Paige for her never-ending enthusiasm and encouragement. Nancy Gershman, for your contributions to the book and all the wonderful gifts you give to others. Kathie Fulgham, for your kind support and willingness to share your wisdom. Penny, for her artwork, creativity, and contributions to Artemecia Press. Darlene, a true heroine and living example of fortitude, compassion, and grace.

My mom, Janice Smith, for her humor and undying faith in me, even in my darkest hours. My dad, Steve Smith, for his support, enthusiasm, and living example of resilience. Derek, for always knowing how to make me smile. Debbie, Casey, Milt, Metta, Julie, Paula, Shelli, Mandy, and Barbara for your willingness to share your stories— and your hearts— with me. Madilynn, Gena, Lou Paradise, UNO, and all the people of New Orleans for getting up and second-lining, even in the midst of silt and sorrow.

Introduction

Losing someone you love to a sudden or violent death is a shocking and life changing experience. Your world can feel turned upside down as you attempt to make sense of what happened. Some days may seem completely normal or unreal, as if nothing has happened. Other days you might struggle with intense feelings of anxiety, anger, guilt, or despair. Disturbing thoughts and images can haunt you as you attempt to understand the circumstances leading to the death and wonder how the death could have been prevented. After my aunt died from a terrible accident, my uncle commented, "I can relate to the Greek tragedies where men are in such gut-wrenching pain that they rip off their clothes. Wrenching really is the right word for it."

You may feel isolated when friends do not know how to respond, or family members distance or bring up old conflicts. There is a strong yearning to connect with your deceased loved one and know that he or she is okay, especially if there were unresolved issues before the death. You could also be dealing with legal investigations, insurance challenges, and media attention that further complicate things.

Traumatic grief can also occur after a series of sudden losses. This happened to me, which prompted me to write this book. In 2005, following a year of agonizing infertility treatments, I lost multiple pregnancies and was told I would never be able to have children. I tried to reason my way through the grief and hide my pain from friends, but deep down I ached with sorrow, anger, and confusion. My husband patiently supported me as best he could, but a few months later, his mother died, leaving him grief stricken.

Right after my mother-in-law's death, my aunt was run over and killed by a large truck while crossing a street in downtown Seattle. My family was already preparing themselves for the passing of another aunt who had terminal cancer. So the shock of Aunt Bev's death was doubly difficult. Nonetheless, I soldiered on until August, when Hurricane Katrina hit New Orleans. As the levies broke down, my emotional levies broke down too. I was flooded with pain, tears, and nightmares for weeks. New Orleans had been my home for several years while I was pursuing my graduate degree in counseling, and I deeply loved her. I worked with inner-city families caught up in gang violence and poverty in New Orleans, and I deeply loved them too. These were the same families being interviewed at the Superdome on the nightly news. I watched in horror as reporters showed people lying dead in the street, violent assaults, and unanswered pleas for help.

Traumatic grief was also showing up more frequently in my therapy practice. More and more I began to see clients overcome with anxiety and depression after losing loved ones to suicide, accidents, violence, or war. Even if the death happened years ago, grief's shadow was still looming over their lives and they desperately wanted peace.

Tragic losses then began to strike my friends. A close friend's father fatally shot her brother and then killed himself. Next, a friend of my husband's was killed when he stopped to help somebody on the side of the road. Another friend's father died suddenly from anaphylactic shock after taking an over-the-counter medicine. I wanted to help these friends, but often felt as helpless as they did.

Determined to find a way to help people cope with sudden, traumatic losses, I scoured books and research regarding effective ways to heal from these tragedies and pursued advanced training in the treatment of grief and trauma. I learned that you do not have to sit passively and let time pass in order to heal. There are tools you can use and steps you can take to relieve the pain and create new meaning in your life. I have written this book to share an approach to healing based on what I have learned from recent advances in trauma and grief treatment, and most important, what I have learned from my clients as we've used and refined this approach over the last several years.

In Chapter 1, I describe *The Experience of Traumatic Grief*, because many people who are going through this type of bereavement wonder if what they are experiencing is "normal." While everyone's grief process is unique, this chapter will give you a sense of what is typical and reassure you that you are not alone in your experience.

In Chapter 2, *Overview of EMERGE and the Science Behind It*, I present an overview of an approach for transforming traumatic grief that I call EMERGE. I use the acronym, EMERGE, for six steps you can use to move from grief to peace. These steps are: 1) Engaging mindfulness,

2) Making living stories, 3) Envisioning connection, 4) Reprocessing traumatic memories, 5) Generating new meanings, and 6) Establishing community. You will also learn about research that supports the effectiveness of each of these steps.

In Chapter 3, *Engaging Mindfulness*, you will learn mindfulness, breathing, and meditation tools that will help you manage intense waves of emotion and ground you when you are feeling numb or detached. You will also learn the value of giving yourself permission to slow down and focus on only one thing at a time.

Chapter 4, *Making Living Stories*, gives you several ways to positively reminisce and create meaningful stories that highlight your loved one's special qualities and gifts. This is a beneficial process because when someone dies traumatically, their "dying" story tends to become larger than their living story. Doing the activities in this chapter will bring your loved one's living story back to the forefront.

Chapter 5, *Envisioning Connection*, you will learn several ways to envision ongoing connection to your loved one, redefine your relationship with them, and feel comforted when you think of them.

In Chapter 6, *Reprocessing Traumatic Memories*, you will learn how to stop disturbing images, painful memories, and nightmares from haunting you.

In Chapter 7, *Generating New Meanings*, you will learn that the way we make meaning of our lives after a loss is strongly correlated with how well we adjust. This chapter helps you expose and revise unhelpful meanings that you may have associated with the loss and consider ways to create new meaning in your life.

Chapter 8, *Establishing Community*, addresses the value of having social support and connecting to something larger than yourself. Although social support is frequently touted as an antidote to depression and prolonged grief, reaching out for social support when you are grieving is hard. This chapter discusses ways to get the support you want and provides a list of helpful resources.

Chapter 9, *EMERGE: A Light for the Darkness*, summarizes the steps of EMERGE, comparing the process of emerging from the heavy cocoon of grief to the process of the butterfly emerging from a chrysalis. You too will emerge like the butterfly, transformed into something different—but beautiful. The steps of EMERGE will help you find your way through this process.

✖

Chapter 1:
The Experience of
Traumatic Grief

Although traumatic grief has some similarities to the grief one feels after an expected death, the sudden or violent death of a loved one challenges and changes every aspect of a person's life. Priorities change, beliefs change, relationships change, and as one griever noted, "Your whole identity changes."

Lydia's story illustrates the way traumatic grief creeps into every area of a person's life and possesses it. An endocrinologist referred Lydia to me for counseling, explaining that ever since her son died from a drug overdose, Lydia had been slowly destroying herself with out-of-control eating binges that were wreaking havoc with her diabetes.

In our first session, Lydia admitted to her out-of-control behavior, explaining that it simultaneously helped numb the pain of her grief and served as a form of self-punishment. She blamed herself for her son's overdose and had been preoccupied with guilt, nightmares, and intrusive images of the way he died for the past three years.

The late-night binges had been the only way she'd found to distract herself from the horrific images and emotional pain she'd been feeling.

Although siblings and friends offered to help Lydia right after her son's death, several of these people distanced from Lydia after the first month, not knowing how to comfort her. Lydia's husband had also been supportive initially, but then he suffered a back injury and became very dependent on Lydia. She rose to the occasion becoming the primary breadwinner, taking care of her husband, and maintaining her home. Eventually, Lydia became physically exhausted, emotionally depleted, and unable to sustain her marriage or her job.

As I listened to Lydia tell her story, I also noticed the telltale signs of frozen, traumatic grief that prevented her from moving forward: experiences of shock and unreality; unrelenting waves of guilt, anger, and anxiety; continuous yearning and searching behaviors; haunting images and thoughts; and a sense of isolation and disconnection.

Experiences of Shock and Unreality

Shock is common in the initial days and weeks after a loved one dies suddenly. Although people grieving the progressive, natural death of a loved one may feel shock too, the experience is often more dramatic for grievers who have not had time to prepare for the death. The shock can provide a buffer, allowing grievers to function while slowly integrating the reality of the loss into their lives. Often grievers will continue normal everyday activities rather than focus too much on the loss. For instance, after one of my closest friends lost her father and brother in a murder-suicide incident, she found it helpful to keep working. She told me:

My clients and co-workers were shocked when I came back to work and feared I was not dealing with my grief. But going to work every day was my way of dealing with it. I needed to have some sense of normalcy and order in my life after something so chaotic happened. For a while, I wondered if something was wrong with me because I wasn't crying. I feared I was broken. But I realized my job and my home were all I had, and if I lost those, I'd have nothing. I had to stay focused on what was still going right in my life and not let the grief consume me.

My cousin noted the same sense of unreality even years after my Aunt Bev was killed. Recently I asked her if I could interview her about her experience of traumatic loss. At first she didn't think she had anything to say, but then a vivid memory flashed in her mind:

It happened so fast and was so out of the realm of everyday that it's hard to think of it as real. I mean, Bev's legs were severed up to her frigging thighs! It was so gruesome, how do you put that in a normal brain framework? On one hand, we're not made to handle radical change that quickly. On the other hand, we are; we put it in a separate part of our brain marked, 'Really unthinkable, weird stuff that does not compute in normal life,' and there it pretty much stays.

Waves of Guilt, Anger, and Anxiety

In between moments of shock and unreality, grievers often experience extreme waves of emotion and even physical pain as they adapt to the loss. Although early grief theorists proposed that the process of grief occurs in five stages, current grief researchers, like Stroebe and Schut, have observed that the experience of grief actually vacillates between crushing waves of emotion associated with the loss and periods of distraction from the loss. People— grievers or their friends— can be disoriented by this vacillation between such dramatically different emotional states after the death of a loved one.

In his book, *The Other Side of Sadness*, Columbia University professor and grief researcher George Bonanno explains that we are wired to grieve in this oscillatory pattern. He states, "Bereavement is essentially a stress reaction, an attempt by our minds and bodies to deal with the perception of a threat to our well-being…. Grief is tolerable, actually, only because it comes and goes in kind of an oscillation." For those experiencing grief after a sudden or violent death, I've noticed emotional waves of guilt, anger, and anxiety to be the most overwhelming.

Waves of Guilt

Guilt can be especially persistent following a traumatic loss. As loved ones continuously review the circumstances around the death, they often mistakenly assume that they contributed to the death or could have somehow prevented it. I frequently hear clients say, "It's my fault he died. I should have done more for him. I wasn't a good enough… (parent, sibling, daughter, son, friend, etc.)."

For instance, Kyle was caring for his mother after she suffered massive injuries in a car accident. One day his mother said she was feeling hungry and asked Kyle if he would pick up some things at the grocery store and stop by a local Chinese restaurant to get her some egg drop soup. When Kyle returned, his mother had overdosed on pain medication and could not be revived. He blamed himself for leaving his mother that afternoon and not putting away her medication.

Kyle's father, on the other hand, blamed himself for the death because he had not been home that afternoon. Both Kyle and his father were overwhelmed with so much guilt that they could not console one another and actually avoided each other for a while. Nobody was at "fault." This was just a terribly unfortunate situation that happened to a loving family.

Survivor's guilt is a form of remorse that gets in the way of a griever's healing. This can be especially true if the griever was present at the time of their loved one's death, as many soldiers and first responders are. They often ask, "Why was I spared while my friends weren't?" This thought can then give way to more severe guilt if the griever concludes that he or she doesn't deserve to be happy or isn't worthy to go on living themselves. Parents and siblings of deceased children especially struggle with this. As Lydia asked, "How can I possibly be happy if my son was so unhappy that he killed himself? Holding on to the pain and sadness is my way to prove how much I loved him."

Waves of Anger

In addition to guilt, the traumatically bereaved often experience waves of intense anger. If someone you loved died in an accident or was murdered, you could certainly feel enraged toward people you think perpetrated the death or were involved in events leading to the death. Survivors can also feel extremely frustrated with the healthcare system and the legal system. For example, in homicide cases, the state becomes the plaintiff, not the family of the deceased, so the family can feel angry if they believe they are not adequately represented. Similarly, after a sudden or violent death, anger can erupt among family members as they attempt to sort out the affairs of the deceased or blame each other for not having done more to prevent the death.

Survivors often feel angry with the deceased too, especially if the death was the result of suicide. They feel angry that their suicidal loved one did not get help or consider how their actions would affect their family. Similarly in sudden or accidental deaths, survivors may feel angry that the deceased wasn't more careful or feel resentful if the deceased didn't leave their affairs in good order.

Waves of Anxiety

Waves of anxiety and panic attacks can also plague the traumatically bereaved. A traumatic event makes the world seem unpredictable and insecure. Bereaved parents may begin worrying more about the safety of their other children, checking on them constantly or not allowing them to do things for fear they will get hurt. I've observed the traumatically bereaved are more prone to becoming hypervigilant, easily startled, and chronically tense, bracing themselves for potentially more trauma in their lives.

For example, after her sister died suddenly in a car accident, Ava would wake up in the middle of the night with panic attacks and an urge to check on her parents. Once she found her parents were sleeping soundly in their bed, she would go back to bed and try to sleep. Often she'd be awake the rest of the night. This anxiety and the resulting fatigue often plagued her throughout the day and interfered with her ability to focus on school. She also avoided riding in the car with friends and was terrified to get her driver's license. Although Ava knew her anxiety was irrational, she could not calm herself down. In this book, you will learn some ways to comfort yourself and manage these emotional waves.

Yearning and Searching Behaviors

After someone dies, loved ones often find themselves yearning and searching for an emotional connection with the deceased. However, the yearning can be even more pervasive after a sudden or violent loss because there are so many unanswered questions. We long to talk to the deceased and understand what happened in the moments before their death. We may regret not having a chance to express our love to the person before they died and also long for a chance to tell the deceased what they meant to us. If there were unresolved problems in the relationship with the deceased, we ache for the opportunity to reconcile with them. Even if we think its illogical, our emotional brains drive us to pick up the phone to call our loved one or to pray that we can somehow hear them and have one last chance to speak with them or to feel them near us.

In addition to searching for a connection to the deceased, those suffering from traumatic grief also find themselves obsessively searching for an explanation. Why did this happen? Could it have been prevented? Were there clues that I missed? Who is to blame for this? Such obsessive searching not only interferes with their ability to concentrate on their present life, but it can also give rise to more anxiety, guilt, and anger as their minds attach all sorts of distorted meanings in an attempt to explain things. Rarely is there a simple explanation for any sudden or violent death. Usually these deaths are caused by a complex interaction of events, many of them beyond control. I discuss ways to deal with the impulse to search for an explanation, as well as ways to feel a connection to your loved one and make peace with unanswerable questions in Chapters 5 and 7.

Haunting Images

When someone you love has died suddenly or violently, horrific images of the way they died can haunt you day and night. For example, Lydia was disturbed by recurring nightmares of her son pleading for help as he was lying on a gurney being rolled into a burning furnace. Her son's body had been cremated, and while Lydia knew intellectually that he did not suffer during the cremation, the dream was symbolic of her fear that he was still suffering and begging her to save him from agonizing pain. The images became so intrusive that Lydia could not concentrate at work or sleep through the night. She was prescribed an antidepressant as well as a sleep aid, but they gave her limited relief. So she self-medicated with late-night food binges of ice cream, cookies, and pudding, eating until she reached a point of delirium and exhaustion, and was able to drift off into a stupor-like sleep.

I teach a method to clear these dreadful images in Chapter 6. In fact, Lydia and I were able to clear her horrific nightmares in just one session when I showed her this approach.

Feelings of Isolation and Disconnection

The traumatically bereaved also struggle with feelings of isolation and disconnection from others. They feel emotionally disconnected from the deceased, finding it hard to access happy memories about the person, or finding that recalling happy memories feels painful because they immediately bring to mind the subsequent horror of the way the person died.

Traumatic grievers may also feel disconnected from friends and other family members. People often feel uncertain about how to respond to someone who has been through a traumatic loss. Sometimes grievers' friends say things meant to be helpful that inadvertently cause the griever to feel even more misunderstood. A lonely war veteran commented, "People ask me about the war and seem interested in hearing about my experience. But, when I start telling them about it, they just lock-up and seem uncomfortable, so I usually change the subject."

Last, those bereaved after a sudden or violent loss may feel disconnected from their spiritual beliefs. Many times people feel betrayed by God or their religion as they struggle to make sense of what happened. We are taught as young children that if we are good, then life will be good to us. Although as adults we know this is a simplistic view, people still find themselves wondering if they did something wrong and feel abandoned by their spiritual belief system. Grievers may begin to doubt the existence of an afterlife. As one client put it, "Because my mom feels nonexistent now, I guess my greatest fear is that there is no afterlife and we just disappear into a void of nothingness." I will discuss how to establish feelings of connection again and discover new ways to relate to others and your life.

In spite of the challenges a traumatic loss brings, you will find fulfillment and joy in your life again. This book reveals six steps that promote resilience after loss. I refer to these six steps with the acronym EMERGE and will introduce the steps to you in the next chapter. Subsequent chapters will then review each step in detail, providing you with concrete tools you can use to relieve emotional pain and create new meaning in your life.

❦

Chapter 2: Overview of EMERGE and the Science Behind It

EMERGE consists of six steps that build upon one another, so it is best to read the steps in sequence first. After you have learned the steps, you can apply any of the steps whenever you need them, in a way that makes sense to you.

Step 1: Engaging Mindfulness

As discussed in the previous chapter, grief tends to hit with waves of extreme emotion. Through my own grief and in my work with clients, I realized people wanted a way to manage these intense emotions so they can function. Step 1 (discussed in detail in Chapter 3) offers the practice of mindfulness as a way to pass through these emotional waves and restore a sense of well-being.

Mindfulness is the practice of observing what you are experiencing in the present moment with compassionate, nonjudgmental acceptance. Through mindful awareness, you can learn to consciously ride the wave of an emotion without becoming overwhelmed by it. With roots in meditation and Eastern philosophies that go back thousands of years, mindfulness is now recognized as an effective tool for managing the intrusive thoughts and emotional pain that often accompany grief and trauma.

Significant research supports the effectiveness of mindfulness in reducing stress and increasing well-being. Studies by psychologists Claudia Zayfert and Carolyn Becker demonstrate that trauma-exposure therapy is more effective when participants learn and practice mindfulness skills first. Furthermore, researchers from the University of Florida and the University of Michigan demonstrated that a mindfulness meditation practice of at least 20 minutes a day is effective in reducing the anxiety, pain, and depression associated with grief.

Equally promising, recent neuroscience findings suggest that daily mindfulness meditation can improve the way our brains respond to trauma and stress in as little as eight weeks. Brain-imaging tests show that people with PTSD have *decreased* activation of the medial prefrontal cortex areas of the brain, which is associated with high levels of anxiety and poor emotional regulation. According to recent research by Massachusetts General Hospital, a daily practice of mindfulness meditation *increases* activation in the prefrontal areas of the brain after just eight weeks of practice, resulting in lower anxiety and better emotional regulation.

Likewise, my clients consistently report that practicing mindfulness on a daily basis helps them soothe intense emotions and relax more easily. In Chapter 3, I teach you some mindfulness tools and show you how to implement this step.

Step 2: Making Living Stories

After a sudden or violent death, the "dying" story can overshadow the "living" story of your deceased loved one, making it difficult to access positive memories. Therefore, this step (discussed in detail in Chapter 4) teaches you how to create a cohesive narrative of the deceased's life, recalling meaningful stories from their life and reflecting on what you loved about them and learned from them. Through this process, you can acknowledge qualities you admired, as well as those you may not have liked. The goal is not to idealize the deceased but to commemorate his or her life and to consider how your relationship with the person influenced you.

Ted Rynearson, a Seattle psychiatrist who counsels those who have lost someone to homicide, leads "Restorative Retelling" therapy groups. He finds that telling the living stories of the deceased is a vital part of grievers' healing. Similarly, research by grief expert Richard Neimeyer suggests the therapeutic value of reconstructing a narrative of the life of the deceased and the way he or she influenced the griever's life, values, and personality.

There are many ways to commemorate the life of your loved one. Chapter 4 provides prompts and ideas that will help you put together the living story of the deceased through writing, poetry, music, and art. Lydia, whom you read about in Chapter 1, used her creativity and scrapbooking skills to reconnect to positive memories of her son. Another client found peace by writing poetry about his mother's life, which helped him come to terms with her untimely death.

Step 3: Envisioning Connection

This step (discussed in detail in Chapter 5) guides you through techniques that help you create a comforting sense of a connection to your deceased loved one. I learned from trauma expert Jon Connelly that believing a loved one is nonexistent or still suffering contributes to "frozen grief," whereas accessing a feeling of connection with the loved one promotes healing.

Although in past decades many grief specialists discouraged grievers from maintaining enduring bonds to the deceased, new studies suggest that internalizing a sense of emotional connection to the deceased helps grievers adapt to their loss. In their book *Continuing Bonds*, grief experts Dennis Klass, Phyllis Silverman, and Steven Nickman report data from a wide range of research that confirms the adaptive capacity that internalizing continuing bonds provides. They discuss findings from the Harvard Child Bereavement Study (1965-1969) that revealed the majority of children stay connected to a deceased parent by speaking to, dreaming of, and feeling watched by that parent. The authors also note that parents who have experienced the death of a child benefit from feeling connected to their deceased child. Internalizing a sense of the deceased child's ongoing loving presence actually allowed the parents to be open to new relationships and experiences.

Based on these recent research findings, effective models for treating complicated grief now provide interventions to facilitate continuing bonds between the griever and the deceased. For instance, Jon Connelly's Rapid Resolution Therapy™ model emphasizes bringing the bereaved into a feeling of ongoing connection with the deceased, noting that what is causing the grief is the perception of a lost connection. Once the griever realizes that they have an enduring connection with the deceased that cannot be lost, the grief is significantly reduced.

Katherine Shear, a Columbia University professor of psychiatry, developed an empirically validated model for treating complicated grief that encourages the bereaved to have imaginal conversations with the deceased. In an article included in Rynearson's book, *Violent Death: Resilience and Intervention Beyond the Crisis*, Shear and her colleagues state, "The imaginal conversation with the deceased is a powerful component of our treatment.... The net result of this exercise is that the patient feels deeply reassured and connected to the deceased." Similarly, in their book *On Grief and Grieving*, Elizabeth Kübler-Ross and David Kessler discuss how the process of letter writing to the deceased provides comfort and a sense of connection to loved ones. They tell a story about a woman who wrote letters to her deceased mother, then wrote a letter to herself with her non-dominant hand taking the perspective of her mother. The woman was astonished by the response she received and the way this activity eased her pain and helped her feel deeply connected to her mother again.

Interestingly, finding a way to maintain continuing bonds with our deceased loved ones is accepted as a normal part of bereavement in other cultures. It was actually considered a normal part of bereavement behavior in American culture prior to the 20th century. I discuss this concept in more detail in Chapter 5 and give you ways to cultivate a healthy continuing bond with your deceased loved one.

Step 4: Reprocessing Traumatic Memories

Experts on the effects of traumatic grief have observed that disturbing, intrusive memories of the way a loved one died often haunt grievers and interfere with their ability to move forward. Whether the griever witnessed the death or not, they can find themselves imagining the scene over and over again. Other times, a traumatic death is so repulsive that grievers avoid thinking about it and have a difficult time accepting the reality of the death. Grievers may also ruminate over regrettable conversations or interactions they had with their deceased loved one.

Therefore, the most effective therapeutic models for overcoming traumatic grief also include interventions that help the griever reprocess these troubling memories and nightmares so that they are less disturbing. For example, in his Restorative Retelling groups, Ted Rynearson coaches participants to draw the story out on paper, telling the story from the viewpoint of an objective witness so they can distance themselves from the emotional pain. Katherine Shear's complicated grief program includes a prolonged exposure process in which the griever records himself or herself telling the story of the death and then replays the recording several times until it becomes less emotionally disturbing.

I learned from trauma expert Jon Connelly that the key to clearing the horror associated with a traumatic memory is to describe the facts of the event while remaining "emotionally present" to the current moment. Recent research by trauma experts such as Bessel van der Kolk and Dan Siegel also suggests the importance of reprocessing a traumatic memory *without* emotionally reliving it. Intending to stay emotionally present as you describe the event seems to have the effect of keeping the rational, conscious brain online, so to speak, appropriately organizing data about the event into time and space so that your emotional brain does not continue replaying it.

You will learn how to stay emotionally present as you retell the story (Step 4) in Chapter 6. This step also helps you come to terms with the reality of the death in a way that frequently clears post-traumatic stress (PTSD) symptoms such as flashbacks, nightmares, and anxiety problems associated with traumatic grief.

Step 5: Generating New Meanings

The traumatically bereaved often assign meanings to the tragic event that make them feel worse, such as blaming themselves for the event, believing the world and others can no longer be trusted, or abandoning spiritual beliefs that used to be comforting. This step (discussed in detail in Chapter 7) helps you uncover any distorted meanings that you may have attached to your loss, replace them with a more accurate perspective, and cultivate new meanings in your life. Bereavement researchers, such as Robert Neimeyer and Joseph Currier, have clearly established that grievers who create a sense of useful meaning out of their loss adapt more readily than those who don't.

In Chapter 7 you will learn how new meanings you give to the experience can transform your grief. You will learn how many survivors overcome grief by shifting their priorities or committing their lives to "what matters." The pursuit of "what matters" may come in the form of fighting injustice, increasing awareness about a societal issue, or simply living in ways that promote kindness and appreciation for human life. Grief therapist Ashley Prend-Bush writes in her book, *Transcending Loss*, that grievers who heal and grow from their loss often do so by generating new meaning through spiritual pursuits, community outreach, attitude changes, and creative endeavors.

For instance, after a rash of violent shootings in my hometown, a group of mothers whose children had been injured or killed formed a movement called "Women Against Violence," committed to helping young people turn away from gangs. Months after her husband died in the 1986 Challenger Space Shuttle accident, June Scobee Rodgers started the Challenger Education Centers for young people, continuing the Challenger crew's mission to educate kids about science and space exploration.

You do not have to do anything on this large of a scale to create new meaning in your life. You can renew your life in smaller, simpler ways too. Chapter 7 will give you some ideas for ways you can do this.

Step 6: Establishing Community

This step (discussed in detail in Chapter 8) teaches ways to shore up social support. Since the 1990's, grief research has documented the positive effect of social support in mollifying stress reactions and preventing prolonged grief. Studies also show that social support is a good buffer to post-traumatic stress. For example, a 2010 study by researchers from the University of London's Institute of

Psychiatry found that social support was associated with significantly greater improvement in the reduction of post-traumatic stress compared to other interventions. In spite of these positive benefits, many grievers struggle with accessing social support after a traumatic loss.

Some social withdrawal is normal during grieving, because it allows grievers space to tend to their emotions, reflect on the loss, and restore their energy. On the other hand, sometimes grievers isolate because they do not feel understood by their friends or fear they will burden their friends. The friends of the griever may also draw back because they are not sure what to do or are waiting for the griever to initiate contact. Through their research in the Network Project, Norwegian psychologists Kari and Atle Dyregrov found that friends of grievers had a compelling desire to support their bereaved friends after a traumatic loss, but felt uncertain as to what to say or how to provide such support.

In Chapter 8, I discuss ways to reach out to your friends as you grieve and help them understand what kind of support you need. In addition, the chapter will provide you with the names and websites of organizations that provide support to those who have experienced traumatic loss. Many grievers attest to the power of connecting to these grief support organizations and providing help to others as a way to pull out of grief and bring meaning to life again. For example, bereaved parents have started such successful organizations such as Mothers Against Drunk Driving (MADD), the National Organization for Parents of Murdered Children, and the National Resource Center for suicide prevention. I explore these options, as well as simpler, smaller steps you can take to establish community.

While helping others and connecting to a community can be a powerful antidote to traumatic stress and grief, it is a process that gradually evolves over time. Many grievers feel too emotionally overwhelmed and physically depleted to actively participate in these activities during the first year or two after a traumatic death. Therefore, I also discuss the importance of finding a balance between healing from your loss and gradually establishing the connection to a community in which you feel comfortable.

There is no denying that traumatic grief is painful. However, you can achieve peace and meaning in life again after your traumatic loss. The chapters that follow present the EMERGE process in detail, giving you the tools to work through each step.

Chapter 3:
Engaging Mindfulness

"You can't stop the waves,
but you can learn to surf."

Jon Kabbat-Zinn,
Wherever You Go There You Are

Losing a loved one is often compared to the experience of losing a limb, as if a part of you has been surgically removed. In addition to emotional pain, you may feel actual physical pain and exhaustion. In their book, *I Wasn't Ready to Say Goodbye*, Brooke Noel and Pamela Blair actually advise the traumatically bereaved to slow down and care for themselves just as they would if they were recovering from a major surgery.

In addition, current research suggests that grievers do not necessarily move through grief in a series of stages, but instead experience grief in recurring cycles of waves. There are high tides, during which emotions are intense and the griever is preoccupied with feelings and thoughts around the loss, alternating with restorative tides, during which the griever is more focused on restructuring and adapting to life without the deceased. Although these cycles are normal and decrease in intensity over time, grievers often feel disoriented by the vacillating emotions and wonder how to cope with them.

The practice of mindfulness lends itself to coping with pain, fatigue, and emotional waves. Mindfulness is essentially slowing down, bringing your awareness fully into the present moment, and observing whatever you are experiencing with an attitude of openness, compassion, and acceptance. Mindfulness not only helps you cope with strong emotions, but it also helps you focus and reconnect with life when you are feeling numb or detached. In his book, *Grieving Mindfully*, psychologist Sameet Kumar writes, "Grieving mindfully can be understood as making the decision to allow yourself to mourn, and to fully experience the lessons of grief with the goal of living life better.... grief only serves to highlight the depth of our capacity to love and be loved."

Using Mindfulness to Manage Emotions

Mindfulness is an excellent tool to care for your emotions. You may attempt to cope with painful emotions by avoiding them, but actually, compassionately attending to your emotions brings clarity and peace.

As uncomfortable as they may be, emotions really are your friends. Emotions are your mind and body's way of getting you to do something it thinks would be useful for your survival. When you feel the sadness of grief, it is the mind's way of getting you to slow down, reflect, and get in touch with the love and meaning attached to your relationship with the deceased. When you feel anger or fear, it is your mind and body's effort to fight or get away from something it perceives as dangerous. When you feel excitement at the sight of seeing someone you like, it is your mind's request to move toward that person.

If you blindly react to your emotions without considering the consequences of your actions, you could make the situation worse. On the other hand, if you ignore an emotion, the mind can intensify the emotion or manifest it in the form of physical ailments. Conversely, when you pause and tune into your emotions mindfully, you gain a deeper understanding of your feelings and can better determine how to calm the emotional energy or channel it into something useful.

For instance, one afternoon Whitney realized she was feeling irritable and defensive and was experiencing tense pain in her upper back. She stopped what she was doing and practiced mindful breathing with an attitude of openness and curiosity toward her feelings. Within a few minutes, Whitney realized her irritability was due to feeling verbally attacked by a family member, and that her back pain was caused by the tension she'd been holding as she "kept her back up" against further attack from this person. Whitney continued to breathe mindfully as she focused on compassionate acceptance toward her feelings and the family member's behavior. Within a few moments, this nonjudgmental awareness lead her to realize the family member really felt as scared and hurt as Whitney. Whitney still did not like the person's behavior, but felt less angry about it. She brought her awareness back to her breathing and the present moment, aware that no actual threat existed, just a misunderstanding. As she continued mindful breathing, Whitney noticed her anger softened into sadness, and then melted into a feeling of compassion; at that moment the tension in her back released.

In his book, *Living Buddha, Living Christ*, Thich Nhat Hanh, states, "...the art of mindful breathing is crucial for knowing how to take care of our emotions." He likens the practice of mindful breathing to the way a mother might hold and comfort a crying child. On the next page is an example of a mindful breath practice you can use to care for and steady your emotions.

Mindful Breath Practice

Begin by noticing the rhythm of your breath without changing it. Place your hand on your belly and feel the expansion of your abdomen as you inhale. Now feel the softening of your abdomen as you exhale. Do this for a several breaths, just noticing the sensations in your body as you gently inhale...and the way the sensations shift or release as you exhale. When you become aware of any emotions you are feeling, notice where you feel them in your body, then gently inhale into this area of your body while you say to yourself, "I acknowledge my emotion." Now, softly exhale while you say to yourself, "I calm my emotion." Repeat this for several breaths.

When your mind wanders, simply notice where your attention goes, mentally labeling the distraction as "just thoughts...just sensations…just sounds." Then gently bring your awareness back to your breath and the present moment. Keep bringing your awareness back to the breath and your feelings in this way, over and over again, with an attitude of compassion, patience, and acceptance. Continue this for several minutes or 20 breaths.

The Heart Breath

In addition to mindfully noticing your breathing pattern, intentionally slowing your breathing rate can have a powerful effect on your nervous system and emotional state. You may have noticed that when you are feeling angry or anxious, your body increases its breathing rate. This is because your body is activating the fight/flight response, aiming to get more oxygen into your blood stream so you can run from or fight off a perceived threat. But if there is nothing from which to run or fight, this shallow and rapid breathing pattern can lead to panic attacks and hyperventilation.

Intentionally slowing your breathing rate sends a message to both your mind and nervous system that there is no actual threat from which to run or fight, and turns off the fight/flight response. One breathing pattern that has been found to be particularly effective is sometimes referred to as the "Heart Breath" because it quickly regulates your heart rate variability, which can improve heart health over time. On the next page is a "Heart Breath" exercise that you can use to settle your emotions and return to a calm but alert state of mind.

Heart-Breath Exercise

Inhale slowly and deeply for five seconds into your diaphragm, so your belly rises. Now exhale slowly over the course of five seconds. As you breathe you can think, "In... 2... 3... 4... 5... out... 2... 3.... 4... 5...." Continue this pace, counting through your breaths for at least one minute or six breath cycles.

Next, imagine someone or something for which you feel appreciation, such as a supportive friend, a special place, or a meaningful song. Continue the paced breathing with 5-second inhalations and 5-second exhalations, as you allow the feeling of appreciation to soothe you.

Studies by Doc Childre and his colleagues at The Institute of Heartmath (www.heartmath.org) discovered that this particular combination of breathing and a focus on appreciation produced the most powerful calming effect for participants, as measured by Heartmath's biofeedback tools. The scientists experimented by having research participants focus on other qualities such as gratitude, love, or peace, but discovered that recalling feelings of *appreciation* seemed to generate the best results for participants.

If you are having trouble calling up feelings of appreciation, see if you can just imagine a special place that feels peaceful and healing for you. If five seconds feels too long to breathe in or out, reduce the count to a four-second inhalation, and four-second exhalation. If you are getting dizzy, this is likely because you are inhaling too quickly and holding your breath. The idea is to gently and slowly breathe in a paced way for four or five seconds as you focus on appreciating something that comforts and soothes you.

Using Mindfulness to Reconnect and Focus

Although feelings of shock, unreality, and detachment are common for those grieving any type of loss, these emotions seem to be more profound for those who have lost someone they love suddenly or violently. Applying mindful awareness to daily activities can help you feel grounded and connected again.

After his brother was murdered, James continued to go to work every day, but felt like he was on autopilot. He would go through the motions of getting ready for work and going to his job, but was often preoccupied with thoughts of his brother or the death scene and had difficulty staying focused on tasks at work. He also found he would forget things because he wasn't paying attention to what he was doing. For example, he arrived at work one Friday wearing one black shoe and one brown shoe. He misplaced paperwork and forgot some appointments he had made with clients. Even going to the grocery store felt like a monumental task. There were too many choices, too many decisions to make, too many distractions.

To help James train his mind to stay present and focused, we agreed he should cut his "to-do" list down so that he only focused on completing one activity at a time. I then coached him to use mindful awareness as he performed simple daily activities. For example, he used mindful awareness as he was washing his face, engaging all his senses as he tuned into the sound of the running water, noticing how the water felt smooth and warm as he let it flow across his hands. He breathed in the pine scent of the light green soap, and noticed the bubbles of silky lather in his palms. As he massaged the foamy lather on his face, he noticed how it soothed the tension around his forehead, temples, and cheeks. Then he observed the refreshment of splashing cool water onto his face as he rinsed the soap off his skin. After practicing mindfulness with simple activities like this at home, James applied mindful awareness to his tasks at work too. He improved his ability to concentrate and was able to more fully engage in his relationships too.

You can apply such mindful awareness to any activity simply by attending to the moment using all your senses, taking an attitude of openness and acceptance to anything you experience. This can also be helpful when you find you are having worrisome or ruminating thoughts. Bringing your awareness back to the present by focusing on concrete, sensory-oriented experiences calms the mind and gives you a sense of control over your thoughts.

Lydia also found value in slowing down and focusing on one task at a time. She stated, "I think the one thing that helped me was giving myself permission to withdraw from a lot of responsibilities and just find the two or three things that had to be done that day. I used Saturdays as my day to rest and retreat from the world. Some of my friends worried this would make me more depressed, but I really needed that time to reflect and take care of myself."

Mindfulness Meditation

Practicing any of the exercises mentioned above for at least five minutes several times a day will produce a cumulative effect of feeling more calm and centered. Yet for an even more powerful effect, most studies recommend practicing mindfulness meditation for at least 20 minutes at one time, daily. Mindfulness meditation is the practice of sitting or lying in a comfortable posture while you mindfully observe your breath, your thoughts, your emotions, and the sensations in your body with the same attitude of open, nonjudgmental acceptance as you used in the mindfulness exercises. Jon Kabbat-Zinn states in his book *Full Catastrophe Living*, "[mindfulness meditation is] learning how to stop all your doing, and shift over to a 'being' mode, learning how to make time for yourself, how to slow down and nurture calmness and self-acceptance... how to watch your thoughts and how to let go of them."

As mentioned in Chapter 2, studies at Massachusetts General Hospital proved that practicing mindfulness meditation for an average of 20 minutes daily can actually improve the functioning of your brain and your ability to manage stress in as little as eight weeks. Furthermore, studies by cardiologist Herbert Benson demonstrated that daily meditation can reduce blood pressure and reverse heart disease.

On the next page is a guided mindfulness meditation practice that you can use for this purpose that takes about 20 minutes. You can download an audio of this Mindful Relaxation exercise from my website: www.courtneyarmstronglpc.com

Mindful Relaxation

Begin by noticing the rhythm of your breath without changing it. Perhaps become aware of the way your abdomen rises on an inhalation and softens on an exhalation. Stay with this awareness for a few breaths. When you are ready, bring your awareness down to your feet. You can observe whether your feet feel cool or warm, comfortable or tired. Bring your awareness to one foot at a time, directing your attention to the heel of each foot... then moving your awareness to the sole of each foot, noticing any differences... then become aware of your toes, imagining you could breathe into them as you watch sensations shift and change.

Now, scan from your feet up to your ankles, calves, and shins, noticing any tension or tightness, while also noticing where they feel okay. Spend time exploring each region of this area, one leg at a time. When you observe tension, you can imagine breathing into it and releasing it with an exhalation. But you don't even have to do that, because just exploring the tension often causes it to release and change. When you are ready, slowly move your attention into your knees and thighs, curiously observing where they feel sore or relaxed or okay. Breathe into your upper legs, accepting all the sensations as they are, not judging them as good, bad, right, or wrong.

From your legs, move your attention into your hips and low back, just noticing the sensations there. Noting where things are quiet and comfortable while sending an attitude of loving-kindness as you gently breathe into any areas that feel tense, tight, or sore. You can continue moving your awareness up your entire body in this manner. Perhaps notice the sensations in your abdomen, loosening any tension by taking a full inhalation, and slowly exhaling. You may observe physical discomfort there, or not feel anything at all. Just continue to breathe with the intention of listening to and accepting your body as it is.

Next your awareness may move into your chest area. Here you may sense tightness or heaviness, but, again, just notice it while you continue to breathe gently and easily. Perhaps you may even put your hand on your heart, signaling to your body that all the pain and sorrow is understood and accepted. Stay with it a moment, observing that the intensity of emotion and sensation rises and falls. Rarely does it remain static. If you experience tears, just accept them and let them fall. This is just another way the sensations shift and release.

From here you can move your attention into your shoulders and neck, releasing the tension by lowering the shoulders or stretching the neck. Continue to breathe as you feel your body respond to your compassionate intention to listen to and care for it. Even if the emotion increases as you do this, know that it will release and subside. Just stay with it in an accepting, nonjudgmental way.

Last, you may move your attention to your jaw and facial muscles. Intentionally drop your jaw to release the tension there. Keep your attention focused in the present. Notice any thoughts and let them pass like leaves floating down a stream. You can always return to them later. The purpose of this exercise is just to check in, tune in, and center your awareness as you show acceptance and kindness toward yourself and your body.

Noticing the Effects of Mindfulness Practice

What did you notice as you practiced these exercises? You may have become calmer, or you may have become more aware of uncomfortable emotions or physical sensations. Whatever your experience, honor it. Although calmness and clarity are often byproducts of mindfulness practice, they can seem elusive if we go into the practice striving for them. In fact, mindfulness expert, Jon Kabbat-Zinn cautions people against going into the practice of mindfulness meditation with a set of goals. If you go into the practice with goals of relaxing, or feeling less pain, or transcending consciousness, you have just imposed an idea of how things "should" be, and the goal of mindfulness is to observe and accept things as they are. Paradoxically, practicing this attitude of compassionate acceptance of whatever you are experiencing is what will eventually lead you to more peace, insight, and enlightenment.

Mindfulness can seem deceptively simple or pointless initially, but stick with it. You will soon discover it to be a very powerful tool in caring for your emotions and reconnecting to life. You may also be surprised to find that mindfulness helps you tune into special moments that are happening all around you, even now. Such moments are a nice reprieve from ruminating about the past or obsessively worrying about the future. The present moment is the only place we truly have the power to change.

Chapter 4:
Making Living Stories

"What you get from being with someone is the experience. The experiences you have acquired can never be
lost. The experiences you have not had cannot be lost
either. Therefore, loss is impossible."

Jon Connelly,
Clinical Hypnosis with Rapid Trauma Resolution

When someone dies suddenly or violently, loved ones
are often shocked by the horror of the way the person died. In fact, we may be so disturbed by the mode of
death that we focus more on the "dying story" than we do
on our loved one's living legacy and stories. Yet reflecting
on your *living* experiences with the deceased is an integral
part of healing. In this way, you make sense of the value of
having the person in your life and you make the deceased
a whole person again, not just a victim. You want the living
memory of the person and the influence they had on your
life to be stronger than the memory of the way they died.

When I interviewed grievers for this book, they consistently stated one of the most healing experiences is hearing stories about their deceased loved one. After my aunt Bev died tragically, we were comforted to hear stories from her co-workers about the way Bev remembered people's birthdays and brought them cards. Similarly, Lydia said she was always happy to hear someone tell a story about her son, Logan. Her sister Patty told her that Logan came over and took her skating one Saturday while her husband was on a long assignment out of town. Patty had really fond memories of skating with Logan that day and shared many funny things that he said and did, which eased Lydia's pain. She was glad people also remembered these aspects of her son. I also had the privilege of interviewing Kathie Fulgham, who lost her dad in the 1986 Challenger Space Shuttle accident. Kathie said "I treasured stories I heard people share about my dad and wished I had taped them so I could remember them all. Children especially enjoy hearing stories that other people have to share about their parents. Now I tell people to record stories they hear at memorial services or similar gatherings so they can hear them again and share them with their children."

Ted Rynearson's "Restorative Retelling" therapy groups for homicide victims also encourage group participants to spend at least two sessions focused on sharing positive, commemorative stories of the deceased before they get into discussing details of the death or trauma. Group members are encouraged to bring in photographs, objects, videotapes, or other ways to share memories with the group. In this way group members affirm the essence of who their loved one *is*, realizing death could not destroy the legacy that lives on forever in their hearts.

Step 2 of the EMERGE process encourages you to "Make Living Stories," that represent the essence of who your loved one is and the impact that knowing them had on your life. This chapter will give you several ideas for ways that you can do this. When your grief is raw, this process may seem painful at first, but the intention is not to amplify your pain or cause you to miss your loved one more. The intention is to help you affirm and acknowledge the gifts you received from knowing and loving that person. Even if the relationship with the deceased was difficult or strained, you can still discover useful things you learned from the relationship.

Storytelling for Psychological Healing

Constructing stories is valuable for another reason. Storytelling is the way our minds bring a sense of order and meaning to things. Often after a traumatic event, feelings, sensory information, and implicit memories of the event are typically left hanging in fragments that researchers believe are mostly processed and stored on the right side of the brain. Yet, the logical, linear-oriented left side of the brain has a drive to make sense of these fragments and put them into some kind of logical order. Building a coherent story based on your memories incorporates these fragments, bringing context and structure to them, which can help you heal.

In session three of his audio course, The *Neurobiology of We*, psychiatrist Dan Siegel explains, "Storytelling is actually a deep integrative process that pulls our bodies, our feelings, and all of our implicit memories into this larger frame where we're trying to make sense out of a deep experienced reality." Dr. Siegel also suggests that the ability to build a coherent narrative of one's experiences is indicative of a person's ability to form secure attachments with others.

Similarly, grief expert Robert Neimeyer's extensive research in this area suggests that the ability to form a coherent narrative of both the life and death of a departed loved one is what helps people emerge from traumatic grief. Dr. Neimeyer also found that a griever's ability to make meaning and sense of their own life beyond the loss was a defining factor in whether the griever adapted well after a death or not. In sum, you can transform grief by accentuating the meaning that knowing the person had for you in your life. Telling their stories will help you do this.

In the sections below, I suggest ways to create stories through writing, art, or music that bring your loved one's legacy back to the forefront. I realize not all of your experiences may have been positive, and in fact, idealizing a deceased loved one can contribute to prolonged grief. That's why, even though the exercises below intend to bring out positive memories of your loved one, I have also given space for acknowledging the difficult memories.

Storytelling Ideas

Use the twelve prompts on page 40 to write about memories and stories of your loved one. You can purchase a special journal or scrapbook to record your stories, write them in a plain notebook, or type them into your computer. You do not have to do all of the suggested ideas, and you may come up with some better ideas. The blank space in the headings is for the name of your loved one. (Note: if you don't want to write, skip down to the section below using art and music.)

Spend as long as you like on this process, and use the prompts to ask other people how they remembered your loved one too. Even if it is painful at first, telling the stories will get easier and bring you comfort. Remember, the point of this process is to honor the living story of your loved one, creating your preferred legacy of him or her.

Twelve Ideas for Recovering Living Stories

1. What were some of _____'s favorite things?

Make a list some of your loved one's favorite things (music, food, places, activities, etc.)

2. Describe _____'s idiosyncrasies, manner-isms, or sayings.

3. What are the things you liked or loved about _____?

4. What were some things that were unique or strange about_____?

5. What were the things about _____that annoyed or confused you?

6. What kind of impression did _____ leave on you? Other people?

7. List some ways _____influenced you (Mannerisms, beliefs, values).

8. Things you learned from your relationship with _____.

9. How do you think _____would want to be remembered?

10. How will you remember _____?

11. I am grateful_____was in my life because...

12. Things I think _____would say to me right now....

Story Examples

Stories of Admiration

Here is an example of a sweet commemorative piece written by my brother, Casey, after his grandfather died suddenly. Casey captures the qualities about his grandfather that made an impression on him, and considers how he will carry on the legacy of his grandfather in his life.

Goodbye Papaw, you showed me what it means to be a man in a time and place where role models are few and far between. You set the standard. In doing so, you raised ten children who have grown up to be amazing examples of the beauty that we all have within us.

Gentle and kind, yet strong and tough, there was never a challenge or task that I saw you shrink away from. You make me want to be a better man and have done so through your actions more so than your words. This takes real courage and integrity.

Your happiness was so genuine, and we have all been blessed to see that million dollar smile on your face. A smile so true could only be brought on by the love and compassion for those close to you, rather than any sort of material possessions.

I love you so much Papaw. The joy you brought into not only my world but to those of everyone you touched cannot be described. You and Mamaw's commitment and devotion to your family have been unmatched. I already miss you and always will. I am forever grateful to have known you, but for the love you showed us, I am forever inspired to be the best man that I can be.

Your Loving Grandson, Casey

Humorous Stories

Your stories can also be humorous, reflecting on idiosyncrasies of the deceased, while still capturing something you loved about the person, like this story my cousin Julie told about my aunt Bev:

I don't know if you knew that Aunt Bev made the absolutely worst cookies in the world. Every single batch she made was the same mix of bitter lumps of unmixed baking powder, sweaty, odd shaped globs, and she'd bring a plate whenever she came over. Didn't matter if they were chocolate chip, oatmeal raisin, or snickerdoodles (Oh, god. The snickerdoodles. No, they were the worst, because there were no chocolate chips or raisins to hide the taste.)

She'd arrive and hold the plate of cookies to you. "Have a cookie," she'd say, and we kids would have to (gulp) take one, take a bite, and pretend to like it in front of her, without tears or spitting it out. As a child I tried many times to get her to make cookies with me, so I could try to figure out what it was she did. Later, I realized that Aunt Bev's cookies were about the gift, rather than the treat, and that's what made them special.

Virtual Dreams

Another way to create a healing narrative is through a process developed by grief experts Doug Smith and Robert Neimeyer called, "Virtual Dreams." In Robert Neimeyer's seminar, *Strategies of Grief Therapy: A Meaning Reconstruction Approach*, he suggests building a story that reflects your thoughts and feelings around the loss using six random metaphorical elements of your choice. He also suggests you write the story quickly, taking no longer than ten minutes in order to keep the task manageable and encourage spontaneity. For example, thinking about your deceased loved one, you could write a story that uses the following symbolic metaphors: 1) an empty house, 2) a cold wind, 3) a dark shadow, 4) a bird, 5) a bright light, 6) a rainbow.

Here is a sample story that uses these metaphorical elements written by a woman named Michelle, after her friend committed suicide. The story Michelle wrote actually has a double meaning. In one way the story describes how Michelle imagined the shadow of depression overtook her friend and Michelle's hope that her friend transcended darkness and found new life. But in another way the story symbolizes how Michelle intends to use this experience to discover new hope and meaning in her own life:

As she sat in the empty house, waiting for him to come, a cold wind blew, and a dark shadow appeared instead. Although terrified, she approached, becoming engulfed in the shadow's curious darkness.

As she got to the edge, she realized a beautiful eagle cast the shadow. The eagle invited her to ride on his back, and they rose to the sky toward a bright, calming light. From the sky she could see the world from a whole new perspective. Surrounded by light, she could now paint a rainbow, signaling gratitude to all those who loved her, even in her darkness.

Storytelling through Art and Music

If writing is not your thing, you can express your stories through a number of other media. Feel free to get as creative as you like with this process. Self-expression through pictures, music, and other modes is powerful because it taps into the right side of your brain, where most of your nonverbal feelings, memories, and insights are stored. So instead of writing, but still using the prompts you could:

- Make a collage or a scrapbook with photos and other memorabilia
- Write a poem or song that captures your feelings
- Record your thoughts or stories into a digital recorder
- Videotape your thoughts or stories
- Interview other family members regarding their experiences with the person
- Create a painting, drawing, or any other work of art that reflects your experiences with the person
- Create a blog where you and others can share their thoughts or memories

Prescriptive Artists

Specialized artists and musicians will collaborate with bereaved individuals to custom-create art or music commemorating deceased loved ones. For example, Nancy Gershman, who coined the term "prescriptive artist," is a digital artist who repurposes a griever's life-affirming photos, memories, and stories of the deceased into a fine art photomontage (a "Healing Dreamscape") to counter loss and regrets. When I interviewed Nancy, she explained that prescriptive art is "custom-created artwork which re-contextualizes memory, shifting the griever's perspective of the deceased from absent supporter to supportive presence. It also provides the griever with a tangible object that reinforces this shift."

For example the photo below depicts a photomontage Nancy created for Hope after her son Ishmael was fatally shot. Through a review of photos and stories that Hope shared with Nancy about Ishmael, Nancy was able to illuminate the sensory qualities that Hope loved about her son, such as the way he looked as a baby and the way he loved to grill hot dogs on cold, windy days in Chicago. Nancy also included colors and meaningful objects that Hope found peaceful, integrating the imagery in a way that symbolized for Hope that she and Ishmael were forever connected arm and arm in spirit.

In an article, Nancy Gershman and Jenna Baddeley wrote for the *American Psychotherapy Association's Annals Fall 2010*, Hope commented that the *Dreamscape* Nancy made for her created a turning point in her healing. The authors quote Hope as saying, "When I saw what we made, I just got caught up in the moment...It seemed as if Ishmael was here, alive. Because it's physically here [as Hope's screen saver] where I see it every day...He's here and in my heart."

"The Bright Lightness of Koot H."
Photo courtesy of Nancy Gershman

To contact Nancy about creating a prescriptive photomontage, visit her website at www.artforyoursake.com. Another site, www.bereavementartists.com features an entire directory of specialized artists who custom create works of art in a variety of media (including quilts, portraits, urns, and jewelry) to honor a loved one's story and legacy.

In sum, there are many ways to capture the essence of your loved by recalling and creating stories. Through this process, the goal is reflect on the experiences and influences you acquired by knowing the person, and realize those can never be lost.

☙❧

Chapter 5:
Envisioning Connection

"Death doesn't end the relationship, it simply forges a new type of relationship, one based not on physical presence but on memory, spirit, and love."

Ashley Davis-Prend (Bush),
Transcending Loss

In the past, many grief theorists proposed that one of the tasks of grief was to sever connections with deceased loved ones, thinking it was healthier for the griever to accept the deceased was no longer a part of their lives so they could invest energy into other activities and relationships. These grief theorists believed that if a loved one continued to feel the presence of, or sense an ongoing connection to the deceased, the person was not accepting the loss. However, grief researchers have found that sensing a loved one's presence or even talking to a deceased loved one are fairly common and can promote resilience after a loss. At the very least, the impression your loved one left on you will always be a part of your life and continue to influence you in some way.

Feeling a sense of connection is more than just recalling memories of things you did with your loved one. It involves evoking the positive feelings and impressions you felt when you were with that person. You could literally feel as if your deceased loved one is with you, or you may feel as if you are just connecting to the ongoing love that you hold in your heart for them. Researchers describe it as internalizing a *continuing bond*, and liken it to the way children internalize a sense of a parent's ongoing love and support as they separate from their caregivers and move out into the world. Similarly, you can internalize a sense of your deceased loved one's ongoing love and support for you as you move back out into the world.

In the article, *Continuing Bonds, Risk Factors for Complicated Grief and Adjustment to Bereavement*, grief researchers Nigel Field and Charles Filanosky explain, "The bereaved can mentally evoke an image of the deceased as a comforting presence, or safe haven, when stressed. Likewise, he or she can imagine the deceased's viewpoint on practical matters... In this respect, continuing bonds can function as an autonomy promoting inner resource." Columbia University professor and grief expert George Bonanno admits to finding comfort by occasionally having imagined conversations with his deceased father when he had an important decision to make. In his book, *The Other Side of Sadness*, Dr. Bonanno states, "Of course, I never heard an answer, but nonetheless I had a definite sense of what his response was. It appeared to me not so much that my father was actually there as the *possibility* that he was there."

Envisioning Connection through Conversations

As a result of research that suggests internalizing continuing bonds is healthy, some of the most effective therapies for traumatic grief now encourage having a conversation with your deceased loved one to facilitate a sense of enduring bonds with them. For example Jon Connelly's Rapid Resolution Therapy™ has documented that facilitating connection and conversation with the deceased loved one is very therapeutic for the bereaved. Katherine Shear's empirically validated grief therapy also encourages the griever to engage in what Shear calls "imaginal" conversations with the deceased loved one as a way to resolve issues and internalize a continuing bond.

In her book, *Silver Linings*, June Scobee Rodgers notes a turning point in her grief when she had a vision or dream of her deceased husband, Dick, standing at her bedside, "visiting me from a light of indescribable proportion, blinding but also gentle." June said she asked Dick if she could join him, but he told her, "It is not your turn. You still have life to live and things you must do... It's wonderful here. The best part of it is you can take the love with you." June said she woke up the next morning feeling much less emotional pain and hopeful about life again.

You can engage in a similar conversation with your loved one in a number of ways. You can simply close your eyes and feel as if you are communicating with your loved one. You can light a candle signifying their spirit. You may connect with them through prayer. You can visit a place that your loved one enjoyed, or a place that you shared with the person. You can write a letter to your loved one, then, taking the perspective of your loved one, write a letter back to yourself with your non-dominant hand. So, if you're right-handed, write the letter to your loved one with your right hand and answer yourself, from your deceased loved one's perspective, while writing with your left hand. In her book *On Grief and Grieving*, Dr. Kübler-Ross gives several examples of grievers who were greatly comforted by engaging in this letter-writing process. Later in this chapter, I will also give you a guided imagery exercise you can use to facilitate this connection to your loved one.

Imagine your loved one as if they are right here with you, interested in talking to you and comforting you. Recall the thoughts, feelings, values, and experiences that still hold you and your loved one together. Use any method that allows you to reconnect with the feelings of happiness, humor, or comfort that being with your loved one would bring. Below, I have listed some questions and topics you might include in these conversations.

Ideas for Healing Conversations

A. Imagine telling your loved one any or all of the following:
- How much you love them
- What you miss or appreciate about them
- Your sorrow, confusion, or anger about the way they died
- Anything you wanted to say or do before they passed
- Things that have been going on that you think would interest them
- Your gratitude for things you learned/experienced as a result of being with them

B. Imagine your loved one answering any or all of the following questions:

- How are they doing?
- Where did they go?
- What would they want you to know or understand about the circumstances of their death?
- What would they say about things going on with the family now?
- Anything they can help you understand or resolve in your relationship with them?
- How do they want you to remember them?
- What would they want you to do now? Would they want you to make any changes in your life?
- How do they suggest you cope with the situation so that you can feel better?

Imagine your loved one answering you in a loving, affirming way just as they would comfort you. They might give you a hug, joke around with you, or say something reassuring. Imagine your loved one doing any of these things for you as you communicate with him or her.

If the relationship was strained, or your spiritual beliefs preclude you from believing you can have ongoing connection with the deceased, you can still benefit from envisioning an imaginary conversation with your loved one. However, I encourage you to imagine that the person can now speak to you from a place of enlightened consciousness. Think of the person now having greater insight into things, and able to feel love and compassion for you, themselves, and others.

For example, a client of my named Cheryl was having difficulty with this exercise. Her mother had schizophrenia and died from suicide ten years earlier. In the suicide note, her mother blamed Cheryl as well as other people for the decision to take her life. Cheryl could not get any sense that her mother was okay and still thought her mother was blaming her. Not only that, Cheryl had been having terrifying nightmares about her mother's death for years and desperately wanted to feel a sense of peace.

When I asked Cheryl about other elements of her mother's mental condition, it became clear that her mother was psychotic around the time of her death, and was not thinking clearly or logically. I suggested to Cheryl that her mother's behavior was due to her brain not working properly. Now that her mother's spirit had left a malfunctioning brain and body, I said, perhaps her mother was able to feel peace and wanted Cheryl to be at peace too. Thinking of it this way, Cheryl had conversations with her mother that lasted anywhere from five to fifteen minutes over the course of several weeks. Cheryl was surprised when the nightmares receded and she began having dreams in which her mom looked peaceful and wanted Cheryl to know that she was okay, that she loved Cheryl and had not meant to hurt her. This experience was incredibly healing for Cheryl and finally cleared the feelings of guilt, confusion, and anger.

What if I cannot sense or feel anything?

If you are still having trouble feeling a sense of connection to your loved one, it could be due to the way you are recalling the deceased. Therapists Steve and Connie Andreas observed that people who had trouble feeling connected were thinking of the deceased as being far away, fuzzy, or non-existent. Similarly, if the deceased died violently, people may find they are only conjuring up images of the person suffering or looking as they did when they died. But these are images, not who your loved one actually is.

Instead, consider how you think about someone you care about who is still alive, but not physically present with you at the moment, like a friend or relative who lives out of town. Notice how you represent this person in your mind. You may notice that the person seems clear, close, and "life-size," instead of small, fuzzy, or far way. You can probably sense how they would respond if you picked up the phone and called them right now. You can imagine what they would say, how they would sound, how you would feel as you talked. Now, imagine your deceased loved one in that same way. The key is to think about the deceased so that it is sensory, the way you think of other people to whom you feel connected.

Envisioning Connection through Activities

Another way to feel connected is to participate in an activity your loved one would enjoy. My mother-in-law liked the Atlanta Braves, so going to a Braves game always helps us feel closer to her. Similarly, listening to music your loved one likes, or even eating their favorite food can help you feel connected. After her son Logan died, Lydia kept his cat. Lydia said, "There was a whole evening of memories in that cat, so whenever I petted the cat, I felt like I was touching Logan and recalled happy memories of him. Sometimes it was just enough to get me through the night."

Similarly, a client of mine named Rob lost a friend in a bicycling accident, yet believed he was still able to feel a deep connection to his deceased friend when he would ride his bike on a particular trail they enjoyed together. Whenever Rob was missing his cycling buddy, he would go out and ride on this trail, feeling like his friend was right there with him enjoying the ride. This gave my client comfort as well as the motivation to continue his cycling hobby.

Envisioning Connection through Guided Imagery

Some people find it comforting to use guided imagery to evoke a sense of peace and/or connection to their loved one. Below is a script I wrote that my clients have found helpful. You can also download an audio recording of this imagery exercise from my website at www.courtneyarmstronglpc.com

Guided Imagery Script for Healing Grief

Sit or lie down in a place where you can get comfortable and begin by taking a few slow, deep breaths. Just follow the natural rhythm of your breath as you ease into a more relaxed state. When you are ready, imagine yourself in a beautiful place. This could be place that you have been before or a special place that you enjoyed with your loved one. Explore this place with your mind's eye, taking in all the natural beauty there... whether it be water, or trees, or mountains, or a garden... this is your special place and you can design and adjust it any way you like. Continue looking around your special place taking in all the interesting scenery there... tuning into any soothing sounds you would hear there.... inhaling the pleasant aromas... and basking in the wonderful feel of the air... the warmth of the sun on your skin, a cool breeze blowing gently across your face... let all of it lift and support you.

As you settle into it more and more, you may notice a luminous light and a sparkling energy radiating all around and through things. On an inhalation, imagine you can breathe in this healing, brilliant light. The light can be soft and gentle, or bright and energizing, your inner mind will adjust it to be right color and intensity for you... whether it is pure and white, or warm and golden, or iridescent with many hues.

Imagine the light moving through each area of your body... filling your chest and abdomen as you slowly inhale... then releasing as you exhale. Breathe the light in through your back and shoulders... then exhale, letting your back and shoulders relax more deeply. As you continue to breathe gently and easily, you might imagine the light traveling down through your arms and hands... maybe even feeling a tingling there... then feeling it move deeper down to other areas of your body... infusing your body with healthy, revitalizing energy. Feel it traveling all the way down to your feet and toes.

When you are ready, you can feel the light traveling back up through your body... taking special care around your chest and heart area... here the light gently loosens any tight places... lifts the heavy places... and tenderly fills the hollow spots... it continues... dissolving grief's hard protective shell... and mending the torn, broken places... as more and more, you are aware of a safe, sweet, compassionate love shining all around and through you.

And you sense that within this light is the light of your loved one... coming from a renewed place of healing... even if you can't see them clearly, you can sense their intention to comfort you and let you know they are alright now... perhaps you can imagine them gently holding your hand...or caressing your face...or giving you a warm hug. Your loved one lets you know that all of the pain and sorrow are understood... all the confusion and anger... all the yearning... all the tears... everything is understood and accepted.

And they let you know that they're here to walk beside you, support you, comfort you, and get you through.... So you can just open up as they send this healing, loving energy throughout your heart... your spirit... your body. And as you connect with them, they let you know that they are okay and they want you to be okay too. You can stay in this moment, enjoying this reunion as long as you like.

If there is anything you want to say or ask your loved one, you can do that now too. They may answer you quickly or slowly... and it could be in the form of words, pictures, songs, or feelings they send to you... just stay open and listen... their message will come through.

You can continue sitting with this as long as you like... enjoying the awareness of being in their presence... realizing they are available to you whenever you want to call them up. They are not gone... they are not lost... they are forever with you and your heart.

Healthy versus Unhealthy Continuing Bonds

Although the research strongly suggests continuing bonds are valuable, caution should be taken as to the form of the ongoing connection. Experts agree that internalized bonds (explained above) are likely to be healthy and serve as an inner resource that allows people to move on with their lives.

In contrast, attempting to stay connected solely through external objects of the deceased does not appear to be healthy and can actually make survivors feel worse. One woman I know insisted on keeping the room of her deceased son just as it was before he died and refused to let anyone move anything. She went into his room every day and lay on his bed so she could "feel and smell him." But as we explored it, she realized this daily ritual was actually causing her to feel worse and miss him more. We began working toward ways she could cultivate an internal sense of his ongoing love for her and her ongoing love for him. She realized that this internal connection could be with her all the time and anywhere. She did not have to lay on her son's bed to feel connected to him.

Although keeping sentimental items or special mementos are okay, refusing to part with *any* of the deceased's belongings over an extended period of time signals poor resolution. Many grievers to whom I spoke said it was helpful to have a close friend help them pack up the belongings of the deceased, initially. Then, as they felt ready, they would go through the boxes a little at a time. While it is okay to take your time going through the deceased's belongings, it is good for you to realize you do not need all of these objects to maintain an ongoing connection to your loved one.

Alternatively, some grievers have expressed trepidation around connecting with the deceased for fear their deceased loved one might express disapproval or disappointment in how they are coping or living their lives. I think this is an unfounded fear. I believe there is enlightenment in the afterlife and that our deceased loved ones actually have *increased* capacity for understanding and compassion toward us.

Finally, it should be noted that in the early stages of grief, emotions of sadness, guilt, or anger are often too intense to establish ongoing connection experiences. Sometimes the connection seems elusive if we are trying too hard to force it. As C. S. Lewis states in *A Grief Observed*, "Suddenly at the very moment when, so far, I mourned H least, I remembered her best... and now she seems to meet me everywhere." Eventually you too will feel a positive emotional connection again.

❧

Chapter 6:
Reprocessing Traumatic Memories

"It's not that people will no longer remember the trauma, but the memory will be less painful."

Alain Brunet,
PTSD researcher, Douglas Institute for Mental Health

After the accidental or violent death of someone you love, disturbing memories and intrusive images of the way your loved one died may flash through your mind both day and night. Similarly, regrettable conversations and interactions with the deceased may replay in your mind over and over.

Nightmares

Grievers often report nightmares after a loved one dies traumatically, such as the recurring nightmare Lydia had of her son lying on a gurney headed into flames. These nightmares were so insidious; she had not been able to sleep well for years. We cleared her nightmares in one session when I had Lydia replay the dream in her mind during our session and change the scene in a way that would be more to her liking. Lydia decided to change the dream by having Logan jump off the gurney, give her a hug, and say, "Goodbye Mom, I love you." She imagined the dream playing out this way several times before she went to sleep that night. To Lydia's delight, her dream changed just as she imagined it and the nightmares have not come back.

In your personal dreams, you get to be the movie director. If you do not like the way a dream-scene is playing out, you can re-script the dream or replace the cast with new characters. You can give yourself and your loved one super-powers and end the dream differently. Once you have decided on an ending you like, imagine and visualize the dream playing out this new way several times. As you re-script the dream in the waking state, it will also change the dream in the sleep state.

Intrusive Images and Flashbacks

Sometimes intrusive, disturbing images or sick feelings may flash through your mind during the day. Kelly lost her boyfriend to a drug overdose one and a half years ago. She stated, "I finally get to a point where I am not thinking about Jack's death constantly and am moving forward with my life. Then a picture of the way I imagine he looked when he died will pop in my head. Or, something else triggers feelings of panic, like hearing the song that was playing on the radio when I got the call, or driving by the hospital where he died.

Reprocessing a traumatic memory so it doesn't continually possess someone is actually an important aspect of most trauma therapy interventions. Most therapy interventions do this by having you retell the story of the traumatic event; however, there is a particular way to retell the story in order for it to stop haunting you. In this chapter, you will learn how to do this.

The Reason a Traumatic Memory can Haunt Us

When something traumatic occurs, the emotional impact often interrupts the way the brain processes the information. As Jon Connelly states in his *Clinical Hypnosis with Rapid Trauma Resolution* workshops, "The traumatic event leaves an impression on the deeper part of the mind, sort of like an impression is left in the sand if you slam your hand down into it. Deeper mind then confuses the impression of the event with the event itself and reacts as if the event is still happening." An impression is formed as the brain records the sensory and emotional details experienced around a disturbing event and tags them as danger cues. Thus, sounds, smells, visual images, weather conditions, and other sensory information gets associated with the event and triggers an emotional reaction whenever you encounter any of these sensory cues in other situations. Anniversary reactions to deaths and other traumatic events are examples of this.

A few weeks before the one-year anniversary of her boyfriend's death, Kelly began to have panic attacks. She was not consciously thinking about the anniversary of Jack's death approaching, but on a subconscious level, her mind and body were associating sensory cues like the season's hot weather, songs on the radio, smells, and other images as signals that something dangerous was approaching and responded by activating Kelly's fight/flight response.

Similarly, if you experience anxiety, tearfulness, or sick feelings when you are recalling a traumatic memory, it is because the emotional brain confuses what is imagined with what is real. The emotions you are feeling are your emotional brain's attempt to send you the energy to stop the event from happening so you can get out of danger.

Maintaining Emotional Presence

How do you reprocess a traumatic memory so it doesn't continue haunting you emotionally? You describe the details of the event while intending to stay emotionally present as you are talking about it. In other words, you have to consciously intend to stay oriented and connected to the present moment as you tell the story of the event. Staying present has the effect of inhibiting the fight/flight response, because the emotional brain realizes you are in a safe place and there is no actual threat.

When the emotional brain is not activated, it allows the reasoning, conscious brain to stay online and get the information fully integrated and reprocessed. Trauma expert and therapist, Jon Connelly taught me this concept many years ago. Several other prominent trauma therapists and researchers are also now documenting the value of learning to "stay present" as a part of trauma treatment.

For instance, psychiatrist and trauma expert Bessel van der Kolk states in the article, *Clinical Implications of Neuroscience Research in PTSD,* "Learning to modulate one's arousal level is essential... insight and understanding are usually not enough to keep traumatized people from regularly feeling and acting as if they are traumatized all over again." Likewise, in his book *Mindsight*, psychiatrist Daniel Siegel reports his observations that conscious attention to the present while recalling the past appropriately integrates the memory, putting it into proper context.

Why is this? Neuroscience over the last decade has discovered that when our mind perceives a threat, the emotional part of the brain activates the fight/flight response, while momentarily inhibiting activity in the hippocampus, as well as prefrontal brain regions. When hippocampal and prefrontal brain activity are inhibited, it seems to prevent the emotional brain from realizing the event is completed. This is why many people who experience trauma report that the event seems frozen in their psyches, continually possessing them. In contrast, when you intend to stay present it keeps the prefrontal part of your brain "online" so the mind realizes you are just describing the event, not actually experiencing the event at that moment.

Staying emotionally present sounds easy to do. However, if you practiced the mindfulness exercises described in Chapter 3, you likely realized it takes some effort to keep your mind focused in the present. In the section below, I give you additional tools to stay present as you are telling the story of the trauma. Telling the story this way takes some practice, but the results are well worth the effort. I have witnessed phenomenal results for clients in my counseling practice when they have used this approach. For example, after telling the story this way clients report fewer nightmares and intrusive thoughts about the death, increased ability to recall happy memories of their loved one, and an overall reduction in feelings of anxiety, anger, and guilt.

Preparing for this Step

Ideally, you have been practicing mindfulness skills, recalling positive stories about your loved one, and doing the envisioning connection exercises before you do this step. The mindfulness exercises will have helped you develop the skills to stay present, which will facilitate this exercise. By having recalled positive memories about your deceased loved one and having envisioned connection with them, your mind will more easily believe your loved one is no longer suffering or dying. So, if you have not done so, I urge you to work through the previous three steps before you embark on this one. I also encourage you to enlist the support of a therapist or trusted friend when you do this step. Having someone you trust present as you do this keeps you connected and reinforces feelings of safety.

Which Memory Should I Reprocess?

Describe the memory that has been the most disturbing to you, the one that has been haunting you most. For some, this is the story of being notified of the death and the way they imagined their loved one died. Some people were present at the time of their loved one's death and might tell the story of witnessing the death. Others have trauma around having to identify the body or cleaning up after the incident. For some, it is a conversation or interaction with the now-deceased person that they regret. Some have had all four aspects or other traumatic experiences around the death that I have not mentioned. The point of doing this step is to reprocess the impression of the event in a way that does not continue to trigger intense, unnecessary emotional responses.

Ways to Describe the Memory:

1. Tell it to a trusted friend, therapist, or family member.
2. Write it down as if you were reporting it for a newspaper.
3. Tell it into a tape recorder or digital recorder and play it back.

Remember to:

1. **Stay emotionally present**. When you feel yourself emotionally reacting to the event, stop and return your attention to your breath and the current moment. This signals your nervous system to calm down and stop the fight/flight response. This also engages the rational part of the brain that needs the information about the event to get fully processed.
2. **Repeat the story** until you can tell it without getting emotionally activated into fight/flight responses, such as racing heart, shortness of breath, nausea, etc.
3. **End the story with something positive** that has happened after the event, preferably something that affirms you are okay or that your loved one is okay now. How can you believe your deceased loved one is okay now? You can think of death as being something that happens to someone's body, but that death does not destroy the person's essence or spirit.

On the next page are some additional tips that will help you stay connected to the present moment that I learned from trauma expert, Jon Connelly. Some of them may seem weird or silly, but they work. At first glance, you might also think some of the tools sound like they minimize the horror of your experience, but they are not intended that way. They are intended to keep your emotional brain tuned into the present moment, so that it does not overreact as you are recalling the memory.

Tips to Help you Stay Emotionally Present

1. Focus on only one event at a time

2. Describe the story in a "just the facts" fashion. Leave out your interpretations of why others did what they did, what others were thinking, or what others were feeling. You can only speak to what you were thinking and feeling in that moment.

3. Include detail, important as well as unimportant details.

4. Change your voice tone, sing the story, or speak with an accent or silly voice as you are telling the story.

5. Change the rate at which you are speaking. Tell the story as fast as you can forwards, then as fast as you can in reverse. Or, tell it very s-l-o-w-l-y, like you are describing it in slow motion.

6. Move as you are telling the story, alternating the left and right side of your body. For instance, you might alternate stomping your right and left feet, snapping the fingers on your right and left hand, or tap on your left and right legs in a steady rhythm.

7. Use past tense verbs as you tell the story, another signal to the emotional mind that the event is not happening.

8. Tell the story backwards. Begin from the time the event was over back to when you first learned of the event. This is like rewinding a movie.

Case Example

Here is an excerpt of the way Kelly reprocessed her traumatic memory of learning about Jack's death, telling the story in a "just the facts" fashion, including important and unimportant details.

It was a Wednesday. Jack woke up earlier than me that morning, which was unusual. He actually hummed a little tune as he made me some coffee and gave me a big hug and kiss before I left for work that morning. At the time, I thought he just woke up in a particularly good mood and I appreciated how sweet he was being. He was often affectionate, but not in the morning, he usually woke up in a foul mood.

Later that morning, I was at work typing a report for my boss. It was August and very hot outside. I remember hearing a weather report on the radio say it was 101°F outside. My cell phone rang. I saw it was a call from my neighbor, Nancy, which was unusual. I answered the phone. Nancy was crying. [Kelly says her heart begins to race, so she pauses, takes a few deep breaths to get present, then continues…]

Nancy said there were police cars and an ambulance at my house. She thought something happened to Jack, my boyfriend. She told me to come home right away. I remembered my heart racing, and I could not think straight. I actually started to finish my report first thinking my boss would be upset if I left, but I could not concentrate. I needed to go home. Then my cell phone rang again. This time it was the police. They asked if I knew Jack. I said he was my boyfriend. They told me that it appeared he had overdosed on some prescription medications. They said they were taking him to the nearest hospital, but his prognosis did not look good. They wanted to know who his next of kin was and some other medical information about him. I told them what I could. The officer thanked me, and said he was sorry to give me the sad news.

My mind was spinning. I did not know what do to first. My boss was in a meeting, so I went to my co-worker Lynn, sobbing as I tried to get it out. She took my shaky hands and held them as I tried to speak. She told me not to worry, that she would tell my boss, and to go ahead and leave. I remember feeling totally disoriented as I walked to my car. It was so hot, and my steering wheel felt like it was on fire. I could barely touch it. So I just turned on the car and let the air conditioning run while I cried. I wondered how I did not see this coming. I knew Jack was depressed, but he did not seem suicidal, and he had seemed so happy and peaceful that morning. I sat there in shock for several minutes.

Then, I panicked and realized I needed to get to the hospital. As I drove, I yelled at the other drivers for being slow and stupid. I tailgated people, wove in and out of traffic, and nearly hit a silver mini-van. I parked in the emergency-room driveway and ran to the admissions desk demanding to see Jack. The receptionist told me that he was in the emergency room, but she would not let me go back there. I told her I had to see him and became hysterical. She went to talk to somebody. Then a nurse with long, red hair came and took me to a small, private office. [Kelly pauses, begins to feel panicky again and tears up. I help her refocus on the present by asking her to tune into her breathing, speak more slowly, and alternate stomping her feet like she was marching. Within a few minutes she felt emotionally present again and continued telling the story.]

The nurse told me that Jack had died and that they had notified his mother. She said she could not give me any more information because there was not a HIPPA release for me to receive his health information.

I stood up and yelled, "NO! NO! I am his girlfriend. He lives with me. I should be able to see him!" Then, I ran out of the office toward the elevators. I did not know where I was going. I guess I thought I would just search the place up and down until I found Jack, but the nurse and security guards followed me. The nurse was trying to comfort me and kept saying, "I am sorry honey, but you have to come with me. You can't go up there." I just sat in the floor and sobbed when I realized raising cane about it was not going to get me anywhere.

The nurse and security guards helped me up and asked if they could call anybody to come and get me. They walked me back toward the office, and I asked them to call my mom. They told her what happened. I was crying so hard I could not even get the words out. They said my mom would be there in ten minutes. Then I just remember feeling numb. I stopped crying. I went to move my car to a parking space.

As I walked back into the hospital, I called Jack's mother. She was more hysterical than I was. I could not understand what she was saying. She kept asking me questions as if I had some explanation. I just kept telling her I was sorry and that I was just as hurt and confused as she was. I guess she was at the hospital, but I never saw her. She did not invite me to be with her or to see Jack. I wanted to see him, but I did not feel I could ask her, because she seemed mad at me. I don't think she really was mad at me, when I think about it now, but that's how I felt then. [By saying this, Kelly distinguishes feeling from fact, and separates past from present.]

My mom got to the hospital right after that. I was so glad to see her. She hugged me, and I collapsed into her arms. She took me to her house. I stayed there for two days. She called *people for me, which was incredibly helpful. Those two days are kind of a blur.*

My mom and my friend Betsy went with me to the funeral. There was no visitation. The funeral was tough. I was in a daze for most of it. I remember over 100 people showed. Several people shared some really great stories about Jack. I realized how much he was loved. I am sorry he did not know that, but I hope he can see that now. I also realized how many people loved me. I was surprised by some of the people who showed, like my boss and some old friends from high school. Jack's mother was really gracious to me that day and thanked me for being a good friend to him. [She finished the story with something positive.]

Jack did not leave a note, so we are still not totally sure if he meant to kill himself. We also now wonder if he was bipolar and was trying to self-medicate. Several months before he overdosed, he did seem manic. He had invested a lot of money into a business that he was convinced was going to make him a millionaire. It didn't work out, and he lost everything. I now think the financial stress of that, combined with the depression was more than he could bear. I have been blaming myself for not being more aware of how depressed he was and insisting he get some help. But he never told me how bad it was. I had no idea he'd invested thousands of dollars into that business. He hid all of that from me. He liked to joke around a lot, so it was hard to see how depressed he was. Plus, he seemed to be in a good mood that morning so it never occurred to me he was thinking of suicide. [These insights just came to Kelly's awareness as she told the story this way. Prior to this telling, she'd been caught up in blaming herself and ruminating over ways she could have stopped

Jack from overdosing. She realized she had never told the story all the way through.]

Kelly repeated this story with me in the session three more times, recalling more and more factual details each time she went through it. Then I had her tell the story backwards. By the end of our meeting, Kelly was relieved she could recall the memory now without any feelings of dread, panic, or guilt.

Finish the Story with a Positive Experience

After you've told the story, I suggest spending a few minutes envisioning a loving, ongoing connection with your loved one. This helps you realize that even though something terrible happened to your loved one's body— as horrific as those circumstances were— that your loved one is okay now, and that your connection to them is still in tact. Kelly was finally able to sense this connection with Jack after she told the story this way. With the anxiety and guilt gone, Kelly could imagine Jack talking to her and telling her that he did not mean to take his life, but that he was scared, depressed, and unable to think clearly during that time. She had this deep sense that Jack really was okay now and wanted her to be okay too.

If you do not feel the connection to your loved one yet, then affirm some other positive experiences in your life that happened after the death. Even if they are few and far between, these positive experiences are worth noting. For example, you may recall acts of kindness that someone showed to you, a positive story someone shared about your loved one, or something useful that you have learned since the experience. The point is not to end the movie at the worst place. Find something redeeming about the experience that you can consider as the end of the trauma story and perhaps the beginning of a new chapter in your life.

Chapter 7:
Generating New Meanings

"People aren't disturbed by things,
but of the view they take of them."

Epictetus

One of the most disturbing aspects of sudden or violent deaths is that they seem so senseless. In an attempt to make sense out of what happened, our minds tend to assign some kind of meaning to the event. Some of these meanings can be useful, but many times the meanings assigned are harmful and make survivors feel worse. In this chapter, I address the four most common distorted meanings that get attached to these tragic events and look at why they are distorted and ways to eliminate them. Then, I address ways you can create something useful out a meaningless, tragic event.

Distorted Meaning #1: "It's my fault."

Many bereaved survivors blame themselves for the sense-less death of their loved one. However, when bad things happen, it is usually due to circumstances beyond your personal control. Let's examine some types of losses.

Suicidal deaths

Frequently, survivors of a loved one who died via suicide ruminate over what they could have done differently. Should they have been more responsive? Should they have gotten him or her into treatment? Should they have not given him that medication? If they had been there, would this have happened? If they had not said those things, would he or she have committed suicide? There are endless variations on these questions.

But when someone dies from suicide, it is because the person was not thinking clearly and did not see any other way out of the pain they were feeling. Often a visit or phone call just postpones a suicide. The only thing that stops suicidal ideation and actions is when a person makes the internal shift to fight the depression and seek treatment.

Some of my clients have argued, "But he was thinking clearly and actually seemed quite calm and happy in the few days before he died." This is not unusual either. Sometimes a severely depressed person has been thinking of suicide for a while but has not had the energy to carry it through. When this same person begins gaining some energy, they may seem happy and peaceful because they have finally made the decision and have the energy to carry out the plan. As irrational as it sounds, a severely depressed person is often relieved when this occurs, because they perceive it as a solution that will finally end all their pain and suffering.

As much as you care about your loved one, it is ultimately their responsibility to decide what they are going to do with their life. The Survivors of Suicide (http://www.survivorsofsuicide.com) website is an excellent resource and has a great article titled "Understanding Suicide." I encourage you to read this to further understand the nature of suicidal ideation and why you can be sure you were not the cause of it.

Accidental Death

Whether an accidental death was due to a car accident, undetected health problem, or something else, the key word to remember is *accident*. Although your logical mind will attempt to determine how the event could have been prevented, the fact is that the event *could not* have been prevented at that moment. Otherwise, it would not have happened. A complex combination of circumstances came together that caused it to happen as it did.

Dr. Jon Connelly often uses the following story in his Rapid Resolution Therapy™ workshops to illustrate the point:

A branch blows off a tree and slams into your house, shattering a window. If you got into investigating it, you would realize that not a single thing caused it, but a complex series of circumstances and events led to its causation. For instance, you would learn that the tree and the branch grew as they did due to the genetic make-up of the tree that was contained in the seed. Furthermore, the genetic make-up of the tree developed as it did due to certain environmental conditions in the soil and geographic location. Then you would learn that the wind that blew the branch as it did that day was due to complex combination of atmospheric con-ditions. If you asked your meteorologist friend what caused those atmospheric conditions, she would say, "Well, a series of other atmospheric conditions." You see it is impossible for us to control all the factors that lead to the causation of any one particular event.

You may argue that even if you could not control *all* the aspects, changing any one aspect might have changed the outcome. This is certainly possible. However, as cir-cumstances were at that moment in time, it did not make sense for you or your loved one to do anything differently than what you both did.

Homicidal Deaths

With homicidal deaths, the bereaved also scramble to figure out what they could have done to protect their loved one. However, even homicidal deaths are due to a complex set of circumstances that are beyond any one person's control.

Most people in this situation do not get a warning that their loved one is about to be killed. Even if you think you got a warning, I would argue that there was not anything you could have done to stop it. For example, a client of mine named Veronica knew her son was involved in gang and drug activity. Although she urged him to get away from this lifestyle, he could not seem to extricate himself. After his death, Veronica blamed herself for not doing a better job of protecting him and keeping him out of the gang.

I worked with kids in gangs in inner-city New Orleans, and I can assure you gang participation is a very complex phenomenon that is not due to any single cause. I have seen kids with loving, supportive parents get involved with gangs as often as I have seen kids with really messed up families get into gangs. Similarly, I have seen just as many kids with really messed up families *not* join gangs. The family situation can be one factor, but even when it is, it is not the only thing that leads to gang involvement.

Veronica finally realized that gang activity is due to a complex set of social, financial, environmental, and psychological circumstances. She also learned that her son was attempting to get out of the gang just before he died. He was actually killed partly because the gang felt threatened by his leaving the group.

So where does the blame lie for the death of Veronica's son? Was it Veronica's fault for being a single parent who was not at home much because she had to work two jobs to support her family? Did poor economic circumstances cause her son to be attracted to the financial incentives of gang activity? Was it her son's decision to leave the gang that killed him? Was it the fault of the fearful kid who killed Veronica's son? Or was it the fault of the killer's abusive father, who caused his emotional problems? You could trace it all the way back to the Civil War and farther if you really got into it.

The point is that, as difficult as it is to accept, tragic events are not caused by any one person's action or lack of action. They are caused by a complex series of events and circumstances that come together in a particular moment in time. You will drive yourself crazy attempting to determine the cause of something, even though your logical mind wants to find an explanation. Rather than ask who is to blame, you are better off asking, "Because this terrible thing has happened, what would be useful to do *now* to help people heal and recover?"

The Amish people of Paradise township in Pennsylvania beautifully demonstrated this response years ago when a mentally ill man shot and killed several children at a school. Rather than react with anger and blame, they prayed for the families of the children and the man who killed the children. They realized this man was very sick and needed help. Nor did the parents of the children blame the school for negligence in protecting the children. Instead, they all rallied around each other, then examined which actions made the most sense to take in order to promote healing and prevent further harm to the community.

The letter below, sent by the family of the troubled man who committed the school shootings, illustrates the healing effect the compassionate response of the Amish people had on this family.

To our Amish friends, neighbors, and local community:

Our family wants each of you to know that we are overwhelmed by the forgiveness, grace, and mercy that you've extended to us. Your love for our family has helped to provide the healing we so desperately need. The prayers, flowers, cards, and gifts you've given have touched our hearts in a way no words can describe. Your compassion has reached beyond our family, beyond our community, and is changing our world, and for this we sincerely thank you.

Please know that our hearts have been broken by all that has happened. We are filled with sorrow for all of our Amish neighbors whom we have loved and continue to love. We know that there are many hard days ahead for all the families who lost loved ones, and so we will continue to put our hope and trust in the God of all comfort, as we all seek to rebuild our lives.

(Statement released on 10/13/06 by the family of Charles Roberts thanking their Amish neighbors and the Lancaster, PA community.)

Distorted Meaning #2: "I am being punished." or "I am not worthy."

Similar to the blame concept is the idea that a tragedy happens in order to punish someone or teach a lesson. The truth is that tragedies happen because a unique set of circumstances came together at a particular moment that caused it. I cannot believe that God, karma, or any other spiritual entity spurred the event in order to teach anyone any kind of lesson. Now, many people do go on to create some sort of meaning or lesson for themselves out of a tragic event, but I do not think that is *why* these things happen.

Many of us are raised with the belief that if we are good, then life will be good to us. But this simply is not true. Bad stuff happens whether you are kind and loving to others or fearful, angry, and manipulative towards others. This is just the nature of the random world in which we live. Animals in the forest do not think they are bad if a predator attacks one of their loved ones. Nor do they think they are being punished if a tornado destroys their home in the forest. Animals adjust. Animals adapt.

Granted, what separates man from animals is that we can reason and have a prefrontal cortex that prompts us to ask, "Why does stuff happen?" This is helpful when we use the information adaptively to prevent future problems.

Yet it is not adaptive if we apply it retroactively or create a meaning that is not useful. In fact, attaching distorted meanings can do more harm.

Recall Lydia from Chapter 1, whose son died from a drug overdose. Lydia's son Logan was bipolar and had been in a homosexual relationship before he died. For a while, Lydia wondered if God was punishing Logan for his behavior and also punishing her for letting Logan turn to these behaviors.

These beliefs caused Lydia to isolate herself and engage in self-destructive behavior. Despite being diabetic, she compulsively overate foods she knew would make her sicker. Lydia also isolated herself from her family and friends, convinced she was not worthy of their love. Once she quit blaming herself, Lydia reached out to her family and realized how much her granddaughter wanted Lydia in her life. Lydia was able to find a new job and a new circle of friends too.

Guilt and Shame are not Useful

Even if you still believe you are somehow responsible for someone's death, consider that ongoing guilt and shame are not useful. I have worked with clients who resist giving up the guilt because they insist they were to blame for someone else's death. For example I've worked with people who were driving cars involved in accidents that killed other people; people who have shot and killed someone, by whom they felt threatened; women who terminated pregnancies they thought they could not handle; and people who have said things like "I wish you were dead," to people who eventually killed themselves.

Accepting responsibility for something and learning something from an experience is beneficial to a point, but carrying guilt the rest of your life is generally not constructive. Jon Connelly helped me realize this by asking:

If shame improves behavior then I guess if we wanted somebody to do better we'd want them to feel really ashamed? Then if we wanted them to do really well, the more shame and guilt we would want them to feel? If a surgeon was performing an operation on your friend, how guilty do you want the surgeon to feel as he's making the first incision? Not at all, right?

I had to agree with Dr. Connelly that I would want the surgeon to feel clear, alert, and motivated to do what's in my friend's best interest. I realized the surgeon is not going to become clear, compassionate, and focused by feeling lousy about himself or beating up on himself for a mistake he made six months ago.

You see guilt and shame usually cause people to perform worse and engage in more self-destructive behavior. Even if you do not think you deserve to free yourself from guilt, do it because that is really of more benefit to others then it is for you to mope around feeling ashamed and doing self-destructive stuff. People who perform well and treat others nicely do not do it out of guilt and shame. They do it because they have learned something from their experience and subsequently feel motivated to do things that are healthy and of benefit to everyone. They have moved beyond guilt to a sense of enlightenment. *Enlightenment* and *understanding* are the things that cause a person to change harmful behaviors and show more compassion toward others, not guilt.

Distorted Meaning #3: "The deceased is still suffering or being punished."

Thoughts and images of the deceased suffering can also haunt the traumatically bereaved. For instance, Carmen was stuck in grief after her son Jesse died in a motorcycle accident. Carmen kept imagining Jesse being thrown off his motorcycle, lying alone in a ditch in excruciating pain. She hated the thought of her son being alone, suffering in that kind of pain.

It may be helpful for you to know that when people are seriously injured, the body goes into shock, which numbs physical and emotional pain. Many people who survive car crashes, gunshots, or explosions do not recall the event and become unconscious at the point of impact. In his book, *How We Die*, physician Sherwin Nuland explains that nature steps in when the body goes into shock, releasing large amounts of endorphins, the body's natural painkillers. Dr. Nuland notes that the elevation of endorphins during physical trauma of all kinds has been well documented in the medical literature since the late 1970's. Furthermore, he quotes several people who survived physical trauma saying that they felt no pain, but rather a sense of detached dreamy tranquility when their body was in shock. He also cites research by psychologist Kenneth Ring, who interviewed 102 people who had near-death experiences. Dr. Ring found consistent reports in which people who were revived after being declared clinically dead described feeling a sense of peace and well-being, floating out of their body, and seeing a light that felt tranquil and loving during the moments they were declared dead. It is not accurate for you to imagine your loved one suffering and being in agonizing pain. They are not in pain now, and it is quite possible they did not feel pain at the time of the event.

Reviewing some of these possibilities with Carmen put her mind at a little more ease. She could release the thought of Jesse lying alone in pain, and consider that Jesse peacefully left his body quickly. Carmen commented, "Jesse was the quintessential free spirit. He had been seeking a sense of freedom his whole life. Looking at it this way, I can see him jumping out of that broken body as fast as he could, eager to experience the next big adventure. He would not have wanted to live paralyzed." Of course, Carmen did not like that her son had to die to experience freedom and peace, but she took comfort in believing that her son was in a state that made him happy. She no longer had the image of her son being alone in pain.

Some people do not believe their loved one is still suffering in the death scene, but are afraid that their loved one could be suffering in hell or roaming the earth as a tormented ghost. I believe God is a loving spirit with an infinite capacity for understanding and compassion. Surely such a spirit would have a greater understanding of and compassion for behaviors that we cannot understand ourselves.

Of course, I do not know what really happens after we die, but I would argue that no one else alive on earth knows either. I do not see the usefulness in believing someone should be eternally punished. It makes more sense to me that someone would find healing and enlightenment in the afterlife. I would think that God or whatever greater force you believe exists realizes that people who die from self-inflicted or seemingly careless actions were not "bad people." A person may have died partly because of poor judgment, impulsive behavior, or some mental impairment. Yet punishment is not going to cause such a person to change. Usually love, compassion, and some sort of enlightened understanding are the ingredients that cause people to change.

Even if you do not believe in God or an afterlife, you can consider that we are all just energy in a body. Physics tells us that matter cannot be destroyed; it just changes form. So once the body is no longer functional, where does the energy that inhabited the body go? I think it would transform into something else and continue to be useful in some way.

You may not agree with any of these views. However, I have found adopting more compassionate views of what happens after we die causes us to create something positive and beneficial from the experience rather than feel stuck in fear, guilt, and resentment.

Distorted Meaning #4: "There is no God, life has no meaning."

Certainly, senseless and tragic events turn our whole philosophy of life upside down. A world we may have thought was intrinsically predictable and benevolent now seems cruel and unsafe. A God we may have thought of as loving and protective may now seem uncaring or nonexistent. Activities that brought meaning to our life may now seem meaningless.

For example, let's revisit Carmen's story. Carmen spent most of her life focused on giving her three children opportunities that she didn't have. Right after Jesse died, her two other children's lives seemed to fall apart. Carmen felt that all the work she had done as a parent was in vain. She then began to believe life had no meaning and any attempt to create good in life always got overshadowed by something awful.

As Carmen and I worked together and reviewed events from a different vantage point, she realized these beliefs were not helping her. Carmen was actually not a negative, pessimistic person. Believing life was futile and meaningless was her attempt to protect herself from more hurt and disappointment. But this belief was only bringing her more pain and anguish.

As she began to shift her beliefs, she realized her efforts with her children were worthwhile. She loved those times in her life and gained much from the experiences. In addition, her surviving two children eventually showed their appreciation to Carmen as a parent. They told her that while their lives were tough at the moment, they actually felt better able to cope because of the way Carmen raised them. Jesse's death did not mean Carmen's parenting efforts were in vain. Rather, Carmen had made great use of her time and experiences while her son was alive. Her experiences with Jesse were to be treasured, even if his life did not last longer. The length of the relationship is not what matters as much as the experiences we get from the relationship.

Creating New Meanings

Sometimes people are able to use a traumatic event as a catalyst to create social change or new meaning in their lives. A good example of this is the founding of Mothers Against Drunk Drivers (MADD) by Candice Lightner after her 13-year-old daughter was killed. Similarly, after their daughter Lisa was killed, bereaved parents Charlotte and Bob Hullinger founded the <u>National Organization for Parents of Murdered Children</u>. After her son died, Iris Bolton started the <u>National Resource Center</u> for suicide prevention and aftercare for bereaved families and friends. Now, I am sure all of these people would trade any of this to have their children alive. However, that could not happen. So they healed by creating something positive out of a horrendous experience, drawing solace from their ability to help others and raise awareness about these problems in our society.

Similarly, after working through her traumatic grief, June Scobee Rodgers started the Challenger Education Centers as a way to honor the Challenger crew's mission to educate young people about science and space. In her book, *Silver Linings*, she states, "The Challenger crew was on a pioneering mission to fly, explore, and teach. If their mission ceased with their deaths, then they had died in vain. We insisted that America's mission of exploration must continue." I admire the resolve of all these people to use their experience to grow personally and raise consciousness for others.

On the other hand, you do not have to do something heroic to create a new sense of understanding and meaning in your life. Many people use traumatic loss as a springboard to value their relationships in a different way. Others slow down and reprioritize things in their lives. Still others become more spiritual after tragic incidents or their spiritual beliefs mature and evolve.

Although creating new meaning in life is helpful, it is not a requirement for overcoming traumatic grief. Some people find comfort in simply accepting that tragic, sense-less things sometimes happen, but we keep living anyway.

No matter how you decide to make meaning out of what happened, the important thing is that you decide to live. In the book *Sweet Grapes*, author Jean Carter found that she didn't come to terms with her infertility by making sense of it. Instead, her peace finally came when she simply made a conscious decision to live fully in spite of past losses. This decision caused her to feel empowered, rather than think of herself as a victim.

Finding ways to cultivate a similar attitude in your life can take time and requires soul searching. However, it can be done. It's not that you have to find usefulness or sense in the tragedy; it's about making a conscious decision to recognize where you can still create value and fulfillment in life, in spite of the tragedy.

As you nurture your determination to create new experiences, life can take on a new depth. You will find you are not as fearful. You can enjoy the sunny days more, appreciating simple things in life that you may not have even noticed previously. Your compassion and relationships can deepen and be even more rewarding. You gain perspective, realizing which issues are really worth fighting about. You develop a true sense of self-confidence and security. True security does not come from external factors, but from believing that you will survive and adapt, no matter what happens.

Give yourself time. In the early stages of grief, there is too much pain and confusion to even consider what I am suggesting. You are likely to be exhausted and not have the energy to create anything new for a while. You need time to heal before you embark on a new venture.

The meaning-making process evolves over the course of several years after a loss. I can reassure you that it does come, if you are open to it.

❧

Chapter 8:
Establishing Community

"And help me be aware always that it is through suffering that we humans meet one another... and that life can regain its meaning through that precious kinship."

Iris Bolton,
My Son... My Son... A guide to Healing After Death, Loss, or Suicide

Research has found that social support after a trauma can prevent the development of post-traumatic stress disorder and significantly help people heal from grief; yet, seeking social support when you are grieving is hard. Partly this is due to the natural tendency to withdraw in order to reflect. But also, as discussed earlier, the bereaved often feel that their friends do not know how to support them following a traumatic event. Your friends may avoid talking about the deceased person for fear it will upset you, not realizing many bereaved people like to talk about their loved one and hear other people's memories. Other friends may think they are helping by giving advice or pushing you to do things before you are ready. Or worse, some friends may actually avoid you; leaving you feeling troubled by the loss of these friendships on top the grief surrounding the death.

You may also feel alone and isolated within your own family because every person grieves differently. There is a good deal of documentation about the different ways men and women grieve. Women tend to want to express their emotions, be comforted and held, and talk through their feelings in an effort to make sense of things. In contrast, men tend to cope by problem solving, doing things, and focusing on the future so they can feel some sense of control over the loss. Men also tend to seek privacy when they are feeling emotional rather than talk about their feelings. Sometimes a man's partner may feel rejected if he does not want to share his feelings or attempts to problem-solve and intellectualize when she wants to talk. Likewise, a woman's partner may feel rejected if she turns to friends or support groups outside the home. In reality, each person has his or her own way of adjusting to the loss and is likely to have different needs.

Open Communication

How do you go about receiving good social support from friends and family? Through their research in the Network Project, Norwegian psychologists Kari and Atle Dyregrov found that the bereaved who receive the best support are those who openly communicate to their family members and friends the kind of support they want. Most friends and family members want to provide support to a bereaved loved one, but often feel unsure of what to do. They look to the grieving person to give them cues, signals, and feedback as to what is helpful. Therefore, be assured that it is okay for you to let your family members, friends, and co-workers know what you need. Yet, you also have to be mindful and realistic about what certain friends and family members can provide for you. Some friends may be great listeners, while others may be better at helping you get things done or distracting you from the loss when you need a break from your grief.

You may not be sure of what you want or need at this point. Many bereaved report that in the first weeks and months after the death, they benefit from people calling, visiting, and offering to help with errands or household activities. If you have young children, it can be helpful for a friend to come over who can lend a hand with the kids.

Later, you may not want as much physical support, but find it beneficial to have friends who can just listen as you share your feelings and thoughts. Women appreciate friends who can reminisce with them about the deceased, explore answers to unanswerable questions, or just be present when they need to cry or vent feelings. Men appreciate these things too but may also cope by seeking friends who can help them get their mind off things or join them in working on a project. Grievers also like to have friends who are willing to accompany them to the cemetery or acknowledge significant dates like birthdays, anniversaries, or holidays. Most grievers do not want advice from friends; everyone's grief process is unique, and nobody can really tell you how to grieve or put a timetable on your process.

Your friends need to know your preferences so they can give you the support you want. Talk to them and let them know you understand they may be feeling as inept and helpless as you feel. Then tell them what you have found to be helpful so far. Explain that everyone's grief experience is different and ask that they trust your way of getting through it. Let your friends know how comforting it is for them just to listen without judging your thoughts or feelings. Reassure them that while you may not have the energy to do the things you used to do, you still appreciate it when they invite you out. Ask them what they are experiencing and what they need from you in the way of communication. Straightforward, ongoing communication between both parties in a relationship is the key.

Support Groups

In addition to looking to friends and family for support, many who are grieving join a support group of others who have gone through a similar loss. People who have experienced similar pain have an implicit understanding of your feelings or thoughts. You can talk about aspects of the death and grief experience that seemed too painful or taboo for your other friends to hear. For example, you can talk more freely about existential questions about life, or your anger, or your nightmares. You also have the opportunity to learn and observe how other people are getting through loss. Advice from these peers can actually be helpful because they do have a more accurate understanding of what you are experiencing.

If you want to join a support group, take your time. Shop around until you find a group that has the right focus and chemistry for you. Also, be aware that you may not be ready for a support group until many months after your loss, when you aren't so overwhelmed with your own loss that you can't bear to hear about the losses of others.

Some people decide against a support group because they find them depressing. For example, one of my clients who had lost her young daughter to a rare cancer attended a support group for bereaved parents just a few weeks after her daughter died. She found it to be very discouraging. "It scared me," she said, "because many of these people had lost their children five or even ten years ago and didn't seem any further along in their grief than I was. I was afraid it would just keep me stuck if I went back." Instead she created an informal network of support through a group of people who were interested in starting a foundation for chronically ill children. Not only could this group of people relate to her loss, but they were also committed to creating something positive out tragic experiences.

Online Support Communities

If you are more introverted, or the thought of participating in a group is overwhelming, you can find other ways to feel part of a community. Engaging in an online support community might be more comfortable. Or you might find communicating with one or two people online regularly helps lessen your isolation. If you are creative, you might find that expressing yourself through writing, art, or music and sharing it with others is healing. Several Internet sites share people's poems, stories, or other works they have created in response to grief.

Finding a Balance

If possible, find a balance between connection to people for emotional understanding of your loss and connection to people and activities that will help you create new life experiences. Many of the grievers that I interviewed said they had several different types of support systems. First, they turned to family and close friends who had also known the deceased because these people could share stories about the deceased and provide perspective when the griever was overcome with guilt or anger.

Second, grievers looked for people who had experienced a similar loss because these people could relate to the experience of grief itself. They didn't always find these people in a support group. After her father died in the Challenger Space Shuttle accident, Kathie said she met another woman who had recently lost her father, and was comforted by this friendship because she knew this friend could at least relate to the experience of losing a parent at a young age.

A third support that people referenced was seeking out a therapist or clergy member with whom they could trust to share their most disturbing thoughts, images, or fears. Lydia commented, "Your friends can talk about some things with you, but they don't want to hear the details of your nightmares and flashbacks. They panic if you tell them you are having suicidal or homicidal thoughts yourself. Even if you know you are not going to act on these thoughts, you need someone who can handle hearing the crazy stuff that is going on inside your head and help you sort it out. That's where a therapist can help."

Last, other people found support through getting involved with a new hobby, activity, or project. Gardening or doing something with animals can be healing because they preserve and expand your appreciation for the miracle of life. You may connect with a group that has nothing to do with grief or loss. For instance, a few months after her daughter died, one of my clients found a knitting group to be a great source of comfort, fun, and distraction. She said, "I did better getting involved in something new that didn't have anything to do with death or illness or my daughter."

Similarly, the year after my husband and I had a series of losses, he talked me into signing up to ride with a bicycling group raising money for diabetes. The team mostly consisted of middle-aged men with whom I did not think I had anything in common. To my surprise, these guys turned out to be fun, encouraging, and upbeat. Even more surprising was that joining the group, setting a goal, and raising money for a cause helped me refocus off grief and start living again. The experience also taught me that you do not have to go out and find a social support group specifically focused on grief. Social support can show up in a number of different ways.

Pace Yourself

While these activities are helpful, they require energy, which may not be feasible for you in the early stages of grief. Often people do not feel ready to step out this way until several months or years after the death. Be kind to yourself and honor where you are in your grief process.

When you are ready to engage, you may want to start off with something small or temporary. So, pace yourself and give yourself time to check out several possibilities before you commit to anything.

Whatever you choose to do, establishing community is simply a way of feeling connected to something larger than yourself, which helps you create meaning and a sense of purpose in life again. At the very least, it helps you go on living despite your grief, refusing to be engulfed by darkness. Being around others with that same energy and commitment affirms that light and love continue to exist and gives you hope for the future.

I've listed support organizations for people who have lost a loved one suddenly or violently below. If none of them appeal to you, explore communities that share other interests you have. I never thought that joining a bike team full of diabetic men would help me overcome the grief from infertility, but it turned out to be the beginning of a new chapter in my life.

❧

GRIEF SUPPORT ORGANIZATIONS

Coping with Sudden or Accidental Deaths
- Journey of Hearts: http://www.journeyofhearts.org

Coping with a Suicidal Death
- American Foundation for Suicide Prevention: http://www.afsp.org
- Bereaved by Suicide: http://www.bereavedbysuicide.com
  (also addresses coping with deaths due to murder-suicide or familicide)
- Survivors of Suicide: http://www.survivorsofsuicide.com

Coping with a Homicidal Death
- Homicide Survivors: http://www.azhomicidesurvivors.org
- Nat'l Organization of Parents of Murdered Children: http://www.pomc.org

Coping with Death from Combat or Line of Duty
- Tragedy Assistance Program for Survivors (TAPS): http://www.taps.org

- Healing Combat Trauma: http://www.healingcombattrauma.com
- Concerns of Police Survivors, Inc.: http://www.nationalcops.org/

Coping with the Loss of a Child (any age, from any cause)

- The Compassionate Friends: http://www.compassionatefriends.org

Coping with the Loss of a Pregnancy

- Miscarriage: http://www.ourmiscarriage.com
- Infertility: http://www.resolve.org
- Abortion: http://www.abortionconversation.com

Coping with the Loss of a Pet

- Rainbows Bridge: http://rainbowsbridge.com

Other Grief Support Resources

- Open to Hope Project: http://www.opentohope.com
- Institute for Rapid Resolution Therapy: http://www.cleartrauma.com
- Rynearson's Violent Death Bereavement Society: http://www.vdbs.org
- Shear's Complicated Grief Program: http://www.complicatedgrief.org
- Transform Traumatic Grief: http://transformtraumaticgrief.com

Chapter 9:
EMERGE: A Light for the Darkness

"Before we knew it, a bright light radiated from behind
the clouds of grief to reveal the silver linings
of hope and optimism."

June Scobee Rodgers,
Silver Linings

You had no control over how and when the death you are grieving occurred. But you can control the way you respond to the tragedy and it takes time. The steps of EMERGE provide a strategy and tools to use at different phases of your grief.

In the initial weeks and months after the death, you may experience too much shock and confusion to form a coherent coping strategy. At this early point in your grief, give yourself time and take good care of yourself. This is the time to practice the first step of EMERGE, engaging mindfulness. Mindfulness practices will help you navigate your way through the intense emotional waves and help you find your center. At this time it is also good to surround yourself with people who can validate and comfort you.

When you are ready, you can move on to the next steps, making living stories and envisioning ongoing connection with your loved one. Your relationship with your loved one is a gift that can still be treasured. You can still call upon your memories and activate your connection to your loved one at any time. Remember, you have not lost your relationship with your deceased loved one. It has just changed form. You can still reconcile unfinished business, communicate with them, and hold them in your heart wherever you are. In time, you will find comfort and fulfillment because this connection can be a more pure experience of your loved one's essence. You get to retain what was best about your loved one in your heart.

Having internalized a sense of your loved one's ongoing presence, you can reprocess traumatic memories and reach out to connect to the world again. You will find you are able to tell the story of the death without falling apart by staying emotionally present. You will find you are recalling more of your loved one's living stories and ruminating less over their trauma story. With your intention to stay present, you can open up to a better future.

Over time, you will find ways to generate new meanings out of this experience that can deepen your relationships and give you a renewed appreciation for life. Remember that this tragic event did not happen to force you to create new meanings in your life. You create these new meanings from the experience because it is to your advantage to do so. It is redeeming for you and your deceased loved one because it affirms that their life had value and their legacy lives on in some positive way.

Finding ways to establish a supportive community with a positive focus will also bring meaning, healing, and rewards. As therapist and writer Bill O'Hanlon says in his book, *Thriving Through Crisis*, "Connecting to others and to a future with possibilities is often the antidote to post-traumatic stress." Thousands of people attest to the healing power of connecting to others. This makes sense because the experience of grief is really the experience of feeling disconnected. When you are grieving you feel disconnected from your deceased loved one, perhaps from some of your living loved ones, and from your former beliefs about life itself. Thus, when you *reconnect* with something— whether your deceased loved one, other people, or a cause— you clear the hollow despair of grief.

Life is still worth living, and you will find your way through this if you make it your intention to create something worthwhile and take small actions in that direction every day. You are just like a caterpillar that purposely and slowly makes its way across the ground until it finds a leaf to which it can attach and transform into a brilliant butterfly.

In fact, the metaphor of the caterpillar transforming into a butterfly is often used to give people hope, faith, and reassurance through grief. For example, a child falls in love with a caterpillar, talking to it every day and playing with it. Then, one day the child comes to you crying and tells you that a nasty-looking cocoon thing swallowed up his caterpillar and killed it. You explain that actually the caterpillar is not dead, but is in the process of shedding its skin and will soon change into a beautiful butterfly.

Fascinated, the child watches the chrysalis every day. He gets a little worried as the cocoon becomes more transparent and he sees the creature struggling and then bleeding as it attempts to emerge from the cocoon. The child comes to you again and says, "It's got wings now, but they are heavy and wet and ugly. He cannot fly like that. This is terrible!" But, you reassure the child that the wings are just gathering strength and nutrients. You explain that in a couple of days, the creature will indeed become a full-fledged butterfly with soft, velvety wings infused with bright, vibrant colors that will take it anywhere it wants to go. Two days later the child comes to you excited, because indeed, the butterfly has freed itself from the cocoon and is flying joyfully around the yard, visiting all the flowers. It even brushes up against his face a couple of times.

Similarly something new and beautiful can emerge from the smothering cocoon of the grief, pain, and confusion you have been experiencing. But, it takes your willingness to be open, intentional, and patient with the process.

In closing, I leave you with a story written by Tammi L. Morgan excerpted from her book, *Emerging Butterfly: Finding Life Beyond Anxiety Disorders*. Although Tammi wrote this story for people dealing with anxiety, I thought it also described the way one feels during the process of emerging from grief.

Thank you for reading. May you be blessed with light, love, and peace.

Emerging Butterfly

The caterpillar had done this before; attached itself to the thinnest thread of hope, struggled to shed some of its old ways, and then returned back to life, as it knew it. Day after day it would slowly move through life using all its energy just to get by and yet never seeming to get very far. It led an unadventurous life and felt very low. But still it dangled by a thread…

But this time something seemed different. Hanging by what felt like its final thread of hope, the caterpillar became motionless as it contemplated its world turned upside down. It continued in this manner until the things happening within overwhelmed all it had known prior and slowly it felt as though it's very self was being stripped away. This left it feeling very alone and more vulnerable than it ever had before. But still it dangled by a thread…

It remained, as it was, unable to move on. Afraid of all that it did not understand it became paralyzed and almost frozen in fear. All its former dreams seemed to come tumbling down around it. Layer by layer it encased itself in fear, worry, doubt, and a spiraling depression until only darkness filled its tiny self-made cocoon of life. Feeling trapped within the emotional casing it heard life outside but felt unable to fully participate in it. But still it dangled by a thread…

Time continued and within the restrictive cocoon a different kind of work began to take shape. Life altering work was in progress unlike had ever happened before. Slowly and after what seemed a lifetime the day finally arrived when an opening appeared from within the layers of the cocoon and light pierced through the darkness. After much struggle and persistence the opening grew and was eventually pushed aside by a colorful emerging butterfly. Although afraid of what lied beyond the safety of the cocoon it gained strength gradually. With a new perspective it noticed both the beauty in itself and the world outside. It no longer dangled.... instead it basked in life itself and then it outstretched its wings... and it flew.

References

Ch. 1- The Experience of Traumatic Grief

Bonanno, George (2010). *The Other Side of Sadness: What the New Science of Bereavement Tells Us About Life After Loss*. New York: Basic Books.

Janoff-Bulman, R. (1992). *Shattered Assumptions: Towards a New Psychology of Trauma*. New York: Free Press.

Lord, J. H. (2006). *No Time for Goodbyes: Coping with Sorrow, Anger, and Injustice After a Tragic Death*. Burnsville, NC: Compassion Press.

Noel, B. and Blair, P. (2008) *I Wasn't Ready to Say Goodbye: Surviving, Coping, and Healing after the Violent Death of a Loved One*. Naperville, IL: Sourcebooks.

Shear, K., Gorscak, B. and Simon, N., (2006). "Treatment of Complicated Grief Following Violent Death," in E. K. Rynearson (Ed.) *Violent Death*, New York: Taylor and Francis: 157-174.

Stroebe, M. S. and Schut, H. (1999). "The dual process model of coping with bereavement: Rationale and description." *Death Studies*, 3: 197-224.

Ch. 2- Overview of EMERGE and the Science Behind It

Becker, C. B., & Zayfert, C. (2001). Integrating DBT-based techniques and concepts to facilitate exposure treatment for PTSD. *Cognitive and Behavioral Practice*, 8, 107–122.

Currier, J. and Neimeyer R. (2006). "Fragmented Stories: The narrative integration of violent loss," in E. K. Rynearson's (Ed.) *Violent Death*. New York: Taylor and Francis Group: 3-30.

Currier, J. M., Holland, J., & Neimeyer, R. A. (2006). Sense making, grief, and the experience of violent loss: Toward a mediational model. *Death Studies*, 30, 403-428.

Connelly, J. (2009). *Clinical Hypnosis with Rapid Trauma Resolution*. Jupiter, FL: Institute for Rapid Resolution Therapy.

Dyregrov, K., and Dyregrov, A. (2008) *Effective Grief and Bereavement Support: The Role of Family, Friends, Colleagues, School, and Support Professionals*. London: Jessica Kingsley Publishers.

Hölzel, B., Carmody, J., Vangel, M., Congleton, C, Yerramsetti, S., Gard, T., Lazar, S. (2011). Mindfulness practice leads to increases in regional brain gray matter density. *Psychiatry Research: Neuroimaging*: 191 (1): 36-43.

Klass, D., Silverman, P. R., & Nickman, S. (Eds.). (1996). *Continuing Bonds: New Understandings of Grief*. Washington D. C.: Taylor & Francis.

Kübler-Ross, E., and Kessler, D. (2005). *On Grief and Grieving*. New York: Scribner

Neimeyer, R. A. (2006). Complicated Grief and the Quest for Meaning: A constructivist contribution. *Omega*: 52 (1), 37-52.

Prend, A. D. (1997) *Transcending Loss: Understanding the Lifelong Impact of Grief and How to Make it Meaningful*. New York: Berkley Books.

Rynearson, E. K. (2001). *Manual for Restorative Retelling in a Correctional Setting. Separation and Loss Services*. Virginia Mason Medical Center.

Sagula, D. & Rice, K. G. (2004). The Effectiveness of Mindfulness Training on the Grieving Process and Emotional Well-Being of Chronic Pain Patients. *Journal of Clinical Psychology in Medical Settings*: 11 (4): 333-342.

Shear, K., Corscak, B., and Simon, N. (2006) "Treatment of Complicated Grief Following Violent Death," in E. K. Rynearson's (Ed.) *Violent Death*. New York: Taylor and Francis Group: 157-174.

Thrasher, S., Power, M., Morant, N., Marks, I., Dalgleish, T. (2010). Social support moderates outcome in a randomized controlled trial of exposure therapy and (or) cognitive restructuring for chronic posttraumatic stress disorder. *Canadian Journal of Psychiatry*: 55(3): 187-190.

Ch. 3- Engaging Mindfulness

Benson, H. (2000) *The Relaxation Response*. New York: Harper.

Childre, D. and Martin, H. (2000) *The Heartmath Solution*. New York: HarperOne.

Hölzel, B., Carmody, J., Vangel, M., Congleton, C, Yerramsetti, S., Gard, T., Lazar, S. (2011). Mindfulness practice leads to increases in regional brain gray matter density. *Psychiatry Research: Neuroimaging*: 191 (1): 36-43.

Kabatt-Zinn, J (1994). *Wherever You Go There You Are: Mindfulness Meditation in Everyday Life*. New York: Hyperion.

Kabatt-Zinn, J. (1990). *Full Catastrophe Living: Using the wisdom of your body and mind to face stress, pain, and illness.* New York: Bantam Dell.

Kumar, S. (2005). *Grieving Mindfully.* Oakland, CA: New Harbinger.

Nhat Hanh, Thich (2007). *Living Buddha, Living Christ.* New York: Berkley Publishing Group.

Stroebe, M. S. and Schut, H. (1999). "The dual process model of coping with bereavement: rationale and description," *Death Studies*, 3: 197-224.

Ch. 4- Making Living Stories

Connelly, J. (2009). *Clinical Hypnosis with Rapid Trauma Resolution.* Jupiter, FL: Institute for Rapid Resolution Therapy.

Currier, J. and Neimeyer, R: (2006). Fragmented Stories: The Narrative Integration of Violent Loss in E. K. Rynearson's (Ed.) *Violent Death.* New York: Taylor and Francis Group: 85-100.

Gershman, N. and Baddeley, J. (2010). "Prescriptive Photomontage: A process and product for meaning with complicated grief." *Annals of the American Psychotherapy Association* 13(3): 28-31.

Neimeyer, R. A. (2006). Complicated Grief and the Quest for Meaning: A constructivist contribution. *Omega*: 52(1), 37-52.

Neimeyer, R. (2010). *Strategies of Grief Therapy: A Meaning Reconstruction Approach.* (3-hour workshop with manual) Eau Claire, Wisconsin: CMI Education.

Prend, A. D. (1997) *Transcending Loss: Understanding the Lifelong Impact of Grief and How to Make it Meaningful.* New York: Berkley Books.

Rynearson, E. K. (2001). *Manual for Restorative Retelling in a Correctional Setting. Separation and Loss Services*. Seattle, WA: Virginia Mason Medical Center.

Siegel, D. J. (2010). *Mindsight*: *The New Science of Personal Transformation*. New York: Bantam Books.

Siegel, D. J. (2008). *Neurobiology of "We."* Louisville, CO: Sounds True.

Ch. 5- Envisioning Connection

Andreas, C. & Andreas, S. (1989). *Heart of the Mind*. Boulder, CO: Real People Press.

Bonanno, George (2010). *The Other Side of Sadness: What the New Science of Bereavement Tells Us about Life After Loss*. New York: Basic Books.

Connelly, J. (2009). *Clinical Hypnosis with Rapid Trauma Resolution*. Jupiter, FL: Institute for Rapid Resolution Therapy.

Field, N. P. and Filanosky, C. (2010). "Continuing bonds, risk factors for complicated grief, and adjustment to bereavement." *Death Studies* 34: 1-29.

Field, N.P., Bao B., and Paderna, L. (2005). "Continuing bonds in bereavement: an attachment theory based perspective." *Death Studies* 29: 277-299.

Klass, D., Silverman, P. R., & Nickman, S. (Eds.). (1996). *Continuing Bonds: New Understandings of Grief*. Washington D. C.: Taylor & Francis.

Kübler-Ross, E., and Kessler, D. (2005). *On Grief and Grieving*. New York: Scribner

Lewis, C. S. and L'Engle Madeleine. (1989). *A Grief Observed*. New York: HarperOne.

Rodgers, June Scobee (2011) *Silver Linings: My Life Before and After Challenger 7*. Macon, GA: Smith and Helwys.

Shear, K., Frank, E., Houck, P., and Reynolds, C. F. (2005). "Treatment of Complicated Grief: A Randomized Controlled Trial," *Journal of the American Medical Association* 293: 2601-2659.

Ch. 6- Reprocessing Traumatic Memories

Brunet, A., Orr, S., Tremblay, J., Robertson, K., Nader, K., Pitman, R. (2008) "Effect of post-retrieval propranolol on psychophysiologic responding during subsequent script-driven traumatic imagery in post-traumatic stress disorder," *Journal of Psychiatric Research*, 42(6): 503-506.

Connelly, J. (2009). *Clinical Hypnosis with Rapid Trauma Resolution*. Jupiter, FL: Institute for Rapid Resolution Therapy.

LeDoux, J. (1998). *The Emotional Brain: The Mysterious Underpinnings of Emotional Life*. New York: Touchstone.

Shear, K., Frank, E., Houck, P., and Reynolds, C. F. (2005). "Treatment of Complicated Grief: A Randomized Controlled Trial," *Journal of the American Medical Association* 293: 2601-2659.

Siegel, D. J. (2010). *Mindsight: The New Science of Personal Transformation*. New York: Bantam Books

Rynearson, E. K., Favell, J., Belluomini, V., Gold, R., and Prigerson, H. (2006). "Restorative Retelling with Incarcerated Juveniles," in E. K. Rynearson's (Ed.) *Violent Death*. New York: Taylor and Francis: 275-294.

van der Kolk, B. (2006). "Clinical implications of neuroscience research in PTSD." *Annals New York Academy of Sciences*, 1-17.

Ch. 7- Generating New Meanings

Armour, M. P. (2006) "Meaning Making for Survivors of Violent Death," in E. K. Rynearson's (Ed.) *Violent Death*. New York: Taylor and Francis Group: 101-122.

Bolton, Iris (2009). *My Son... My Son... A Guide to Healing After Death, Loss, or Suicide.* Roswell, GA: Bolton Press Atlanta.

Carter, J. (1998). *Sweet Grapes: How to Stop Being Infertile and Start Living Again.* Indiana: Perspective Press.

Connelly, J. (2009). *Clinical Hypnosis with Rapid Trauma Resolution.* Jupiter, FL: Institute for Rapid Resolution Therapy.

Hawton, K. and Simkin, S. (2008). *Help is at Hand: A Resource for People Bereaved by Suicide and other Sudden, Traumatic Death.* Centre for Suicide Research, University of Oxford. Oxford, England. COI for the Department of Health.

Jordan, J. (2009). After Suicide: Clinical Work with Survivors. *Grief Matters: The Australian Journal of Grief and Bereavement,* 12(1), 4-9.

Neimeyer, R. (2010). *Strategies of Grief Therapy: A Meaning Reconstruction Approach.* (3-hour workshop with manual) Eau Claire, Wisconsin: CMI Education.

Nuland, S. (1995). *How We Die: Reflections on Life's Final Chapter.* New York: Random House.

O'Hara, Kathleen. (2006). *A Grief Like No Other.* New York: Marlowe and Company.

Prend, A. D. (1997). *Transcending Loss: Understanding the Lifelong Impact of Grief and How to make it Meaningful.* New York: Berkley Books.

Rodgers, June Scobee (2011) *Silver Linings: My Life Before and After Challenger 7.* Macon, GA: Smith and Helwys.

Ch. 8- Establishing Community

Bisconti, T. L., Bergman, C. S., Boker, S. M. (2006). "Social support as a predictor in variability: An examination of the adjustment trajectories of recent widows," *Psychology and Aging,* 21(3): 590-99.

Bolton, Iris (2009). *My Son... My Son... A Guide to Healing After Death, Loss, or Suicide.* Roswell, GA: Bolton Press Atlanta.

Doka, K. Martin, T. (2010). *Grieving Beyond Gender: Understanding the Differences Between the Way Men and Women Mourn.* New York: Taylor and Francis Group.

Dyregrov, K., and Dyregrov, A. (2008). *Effective Grief and Bereavement Support: The Role of Family, Friends, Colleagues, School, and Support Professionals.* London: Jessica Kingsley Publishers.

Eisenberg, N., Fabes, R., Miller, P., Fultz, J., Shell, R., Mathy, R., Reno, R. (1989). "Relation of sympathy and distress to pro-social behavior: A multi-method study," *Journal of Personality and Social Psychology* 57: 55-66.

Thrasher, S., Power, M., Morant, N., Marks, I., Dalgleish, T. (2010). Social support moderates outcome in a randomized controlled trial of exposure therapy and (or) cognitive restructuring for chronic posttraumatic stress disorder. *Canadian Journal of Psychiatry*: 55(3): 187-190.

Ch. 9- EMERGE: A Light for the Darkness

Morgan, Tammi L. (2008). *Emerging Butterfly: Life Beyond Anxiety Disorders.* Frederick, MD: Publish America.

O'Hanlon, Bill. (2004). *Thriving Through Crisis: Turn Tragedy and Trauma into Growth and Change.* New York: Berkley Publishing.

Rodgers, June Scobee (2011) *Silver Linings: My Life Before and After Challenger 7.* Macon, GA: Smith and Helwys.

⚜

About Courtney Armstrong

Courtney Armstrong is a licensed professional counselor who owns a private practice in Chattanooga, Tennessee. In practice since 1995, she counsels people recovering from grief and trauma, and trains mental health professionals across the United States in methods of treatment that promote resilience. When Courtney is not counseling or teaching, she enjoys riding her bike and hiking the Tennessee hills with her husband Joel and their faithful dog, Buzz.

To get more tools, updates, and connect with Courtney online:
http://transformtraumaticgrief.com
http://www.courtneyarmstronglpc.com
http://traumatherapyalternatives.com

Made in the USA
Lexington, KY
19 March 2015